For JJ + Helen

Performing Technology: User Content and the New Digital Media

Performing Technology: User Content and the New Digital Media: Insights from the Two Thousand + NINE Symposium

Edited by

Franziska Schroeder

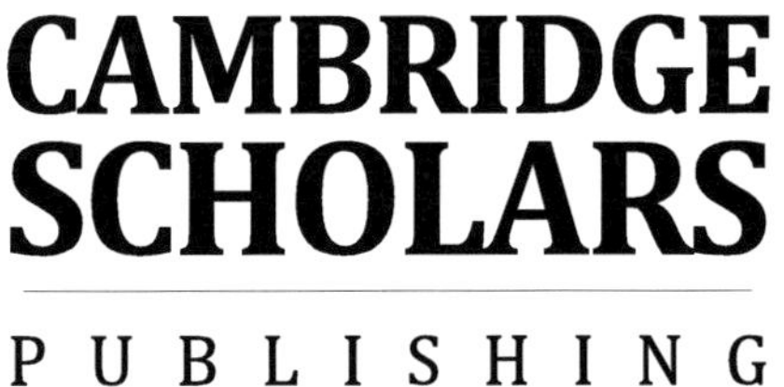

Performing Technology: User Content and the New Digital Media:
Insights from the Two Thousand + NINE Symposium,
Edited by Franziska Schroeder

This book first published 2009

Cambridge Scholars Publishing

12 Back Chapman Street, Newcastle upon Tyne, NE6 2XX, UK

British Library Cataloguing in Publication Data
A catalogue record for this book is available from the British Library

ISBN (10): 1-4438-1445-8, ISBN (13): 978-1-4438-1445-4

Dedicated to the three most important boys: Pedro, Lukas and Max.

TABLE OF CONTENTS

LIST OF FIGURES

Chapter Five

Chapter Eight

ACKNOWLEDGEMENTS

I would like to acknowledge the kind support of Dr. Mícheál Ó hAodha from the University of Limerick/Department of History. Mícheál contacted me in the first place and encouraged me to publish this volume. I am thankful for his editorial insights and overall support.

INTRODUCTION

Dear Reader.

This volume was spawned by the invigorating discussions during the 2009 edition of the *Two Thousand + symposia* series. Since 2006 this series has invited researchers from fields as diverse as music, architecture, design, philosophy, dance and technology to discuss issues around performance and technologies. The series has been running alongside the Sonorities Festival of Contemporary Music in Belfast (more on the series can be found here:
www.sarc.qub.ac.uk/~fschroeder/Symposium/index.htm).

The *Two Thousand + NINE* symposium focused on user-generated content. The writings included in this volume have been selected in the context of this theme. The original call for the symposium was intended to foster discussions around design processes and creative practice strategies. It can be said that dissemination of "content" has been challenged dramatically by environments such as Facebook, Youtube and SecondLife as these introduce notionally open platforms that live off content created by users. Although user-generated content has fulfilled the engagement requirement of many social networking environments, the question emerges in relation to the role of creative practice in a context which promotes malleable, transitory and user-led media. In a world of post-personalisation, digital media is faced with issues of locality, context and mobility. Although numerous applications have been built on creating environments within which personal preferences, approaches or visions can be implemented, the question of how design processes and creative practice strategies address these new media is still unanswered. Presenters at the symposium tackled questions such as how notions of open form and interactive media relate to user-centred interaction design, what the shift from object to environment might imply for contemporary artistic practice, as well as questions about the development of design strategies for addressing rich media environments that incorporate user-generated, locative content.

I have deliberately not grouped the chapters together by themes such as 'dance', 'virtual worlds', 'music performance' or 'computer games', but have chosen to arrange the chapters according to alphabetical order of the authors' last names. I imagine that each reader will be approaching this volume in a very different order anyway; that each of you will have a particular way of reading that is suited to your current interests and research priorities, and with this in mind I wanted to leave the chapters in a more 'random' order, rather than impose an artificial suggestion for possible ways of reading. The ideas and critical positions you will find in this volume are the following:

Choinière positions the body as a vehicle for examining design strategies in dance. In particular, she argues for a new understanding of the body in dance, situating the body (the collective or embryonic body) in states of destabilisation and fragility and thus allows for the deconstruction of the hierarchical body.

Fernandes' and **Jürgens'** work takes as a starting point for the discussion on user-generated content the 'inter-contamination'; that is, the creative potential that lies in the contact zone of various disciplines. They examine a very particular transdisciplinary project, the *Transmedia Knowledge Base project (TKB)*, which serves to document, structure and annotate digital dance pieces in order to examine underlying choreographic thinking. The project is intended to allow for a deeper insight into dance practices.

The co-authored work by **Kazuhiro** and **Tanaka** explores how users engage socially with music; specifically, the authors consider how creators conceive of participatory forms of music in order for the act of music making to become a collective activity.

Magruder's chapter provides a great overview of the rise of online sharing communities, in particular SecondLife. The author examines the architectural theory of Vitruvius, especially the specific formulae for building structures based on notions of *firmitas*, *utilitas*, *venustas*. This chapter elaborates on Magruder's own work *The Vitruvian World,* which is a fine example of the hybridisation of virtual, physical and networked space.

Millward addresses the relationships between sound, moving image and emotive intent; in particular, the author looks at the phonaesthetic relationship between image and sound. He elaborates on his own multimedia work *From Anger To Sadness,* a work that investigates the motions of emotionally motivated vocal folds and represents these as abstracted 3D moving images.

The following chapter by **Newman** investigates the role and place for the performance artist in virtual worlds. The formation of social and intimate bonds in virtual environments, in particular in SecondLife, are scrutinised while the authors reminds us of the risks of love and the future of the physical body.

O'Dwyer examines a kind of collective experience of place by looking at the role of the portable audio device. She argues that the personal listening experiences which these devices create produce a networked, collective experience of place, transforming non-place into a ludic sphere for social interactions. O'Dwyer considers the device as an active producer of place as opposed to the common view of the device absenting a user from place. The users not only shape, but also become shaped by the technology.

Renaud's work on sonic travel in the network examines the design of the network and the rendering of its nodes as part of the musical process. In the author's own work the nodes send signals around the network and thus the acoustics of the network become integral to the compositional design in which the network not only creates sonic reflections but also a complex instrument in its own right.

In my own paper (**Schroeder**) I examine listening attitudes in network music environments. I address the theme of user-generated content by looking at a specific network composition entitled "Netrooms" which relies on the users to generate sound materials that are used in the performance. The main focus of the paper is to contemplate how the nature of the network reveals the nature of our own listening.

Traynor's chapter examines the notorious Oklahoma City band "The Flaming Lips" and their ground-breaking album *Zaireeka*. User-generated content is discussed in terms of this particular user-centred album, a social album and interactive multi-disc listening experience where listeners are asked to play four discs simultaneously and synchronised on four different audio systems. *Zaireeka* was inspired by the 'Parking Lot Experiments' of the late 90s, and different elements of the same song were reproduced on different discs. Traynor argues that this infamous album is challenging our preconceived assumptions of recorded music and listening environment.

Waters' work problematises the notion of content in technologised environments; in particular the author looks at the relationship between 'content' and 'container' as well as notions of noise and resolution, overload, supplement, arbitrariness and mutability, emergence, collaboration, authorship and ownership, and silence and absence. Waters convincingly argues that content is not only contingent on the active input of participants; but also, that it can be characterised as having emergent properties in the same way that a musical instrument emerges through means of its use.

The final chapter by **White** considers video games as an art form rather than as a simple form of entertainment. The author points out the necessity for the tactile engagement of the users and thus agency, and he argues for a breaking of the separation between the real and the virtual world; for the user and machine to be treated as distinct entities that become embodied. White says that video games need to allow for a tactile disruption that eventually can lead to a distinct realisation within user.

As an editor I had the pleasure in collating above articles that represent current thinking across a variety of fields. I have found the articles exciting and beneficial for my own area of research and they certainly have shed some new light on the issue of user-generated content in new digital media environments.

I hope you enjoy.

—Franziska Schroeder
Belfast, October 2009

CHAPTER ONE

THE *SONIC COLLECTIVE BODY* AS A STRATEGY TO INVEST NEW DESIGNS AND NEW REALITIES

ISABELLE CHOINIÈRE

1. Introduction

This article explores the means by which we can develop new design strategies in the context of evolution in actual dance, through the influence of 20th and 21st century technology and its impact on perception.

By applying a performative, adaptive and evolutionary strategy generated by user-generators equipped with sensors among other things, we discuss the notion of an enlarged/sonorous body, of the technological sound device integrated through the development of the concept of the Collective Body. This term gains its full meaning when applied to a re-evaluation of the notion of the Interval, particularly with the dissolution of the psycho-physical barrier that is characteristic of the Collective Body.

We also propose the notion of the 'Collective Sonorous Body' as an integrating element born out of a new way of learning, of a new experiential understanding of the body, and not as ones duplicate or element of superposition. This 'Collective Sonorous Body' is generated by the existence of a strategy of design and creation based on the renewal of being born. Through this concept, we invest the notion of performativity, one experimenting with *new realities,* not the one leading to representation. This other corporality integrates the phenomenon of reality transformation brought about by these new ways of learning.

2. Research Strategies

To reach this aim, we have opted for a research strategy that investigates the manner in which the infusion of technological thought in actual dance/performance could find applications in developing new choreographic/performative models. Our artistic experimentation is based on a strategy of sensory experience and perceptual renewal: how will 20th and 21st century technology be able to open the path to a new perceptual synaesthesia[1] formed by proprioception of the real body and exteroception of the mediated body?[2] According to our hypotheses, this research could initiate a relationship that enriches the potential of experiential corporeality (we propose this approach as a means to move beyond the instrumentalization that diminishes the dancer in relation to technology.)

We also discuss the concept of interval and of the dissolution of the psycho-corporeal barrier – a theory developed by Suely Rolnik, cultural critic and psychoanalyst – as a connecting and integrative learning technique that, propelled by technology, leads to the destabilization of our sensorial cartography. This will, in turn, create a ‘vibratory’ relationship, (thus transformative and inter-connective) between performers and public which will also lead to experiencing new realities. This state of interconnection is also a prerequisite to the 'recognition' between bodies, which itself depends upon the dissolution of the psycho-corporeal barrier. The 'recognition' between bodies would, in part, be explained by the 'mirror neuron' phenomena developed by Italian neuroscientist Giacomo Rizzolatti (2005). This other performative configuration based on learning by direct contact and on a remote basis promotes the experience of a creative process inside a shared relationship and also promotes another design strategy. This interval, in accordance to the Japanese Ma, is a moving time-space, an empty space to be inhabited, *a* possibility. For the Japanese people, all potentiality resides in emptiness, that of *a* becoming. For Suely Rolnik, potentiality resides in the state of fragility, of reciprocal psycho-corporeal resonance, which creates an intercommunication, the organization of a vibratory collective body. This new design process and these creative practical strategies will result in another enlarged corporeal representation typical to the new corporealities issuing from the sensorial and perceptual destabilization created by the media.

3. The principles behind the construction of the Collective Body and its vital link with the notion of interval.

This paper will try to answer to this question : “Why is this question of 'interval' so important in our times? How does the idea of 'interval' insert and develop itself in post-modern *(early 60’s to late 70’s)* and actual/new dance *(early 80’s to present day)*?”

Modern Dance is a *“global designation for the whole scenic dance that has broken off with ballet and popular entertainment.”* (Banes, 2002) It was invented in the United States through the coming of three great women in the dance world: Loïe Fuller, who threw the foundations of Modern Dance in 1890; Isadora Duncan, and next Ruth St-Denis, who held a school from 1915 to 1930. ‘*In the early Sixties, when Yvonne Rainer uses the term “Post-Modern” to qualify the work that she and her peers present at the Judson and elsewhere, she uses it firstly and foremost in a chronological sense*’ (Banes, 2002). Post Modern Dance was invented in the United States and its main actors were, among others, Merce Cunningham – who began, as soon as 1944, to propose an approach which radically contrasted with Modern Dance -, Lucinda Child, Steve Paxton, Deborah Hay, Trisha Brown and Yvonne Rainer. As of Butoh, it can be considered Japan’s Post Modern Dance.

> From the breaking point of the Sixties, time of the Judson Dance Theater where every rule was questioned, to the consolidation of Post-Modern Dance, in the late Sixties-early Seventies, into two main streams, the analytical and the metaphorical – when experimentation would step aside to see ‘identifiable’ styles emerge – we would find the same questions asked by the choreographers: what is Dance? Where, when and how must it be executed? In the Eighties, although “New Dance” choreographers still passionately took part in the debate on the nature of this medium, they clearly distinguished themselves from their postmodern predecessors by their interest in the SIGNIFICATION of Dance. For reasons that relate to history of avant-garde as well as to the spirit of our time, the Eighties witness the urgency of seeking content in Arts, and in this, Dance is no exception (Banes 1985).

This fundamental path that dance traces in regard to this notion of 'interval' – strongly inspired by the Japanese notion of Ma[3] – lies within a profound syncretic process. To us, it is the product of a “cannibalistic” dimension in the positive and integrative meaning as seen by the Brazilian people. The ‘resounding collective body’ that we experiment with is interested by the potentiality existing in the interval of the collective body and retains some strategies belonging to Paxton's tactile body (he developed the Contact Dance Method), Brown's fluid body and the Butoh's introspective body.

The technological times in which we live have broken the idea of distance as we knew it in the Renaissance period – the Times of Vision (de Kerckhove, to be published in 2010). We exist in multi-sensorial universes where our consciousness of the whole is instantaneous (Weissberg, 1988). Technology becomes the catalyst of the sensorial renewal process by installing a permanent destabilization made possible by electronic media due to the fact that several universes have moved closer together (Rolnik, Figures nouvelles du chaos, 2007). What ensues is a constant reorganization of our senses among themselves – our sensorial mappings – where we find ourselves in an exacerbated state of being, of life, of "presence"; a state of openness and sensorial and perceptual listening which Suely Rolnik names "state of fragility" – a state which results from these reorganizations – and which will become the condition for the experiential state. This state of fragility is essential in order to permit the "vibratory" (Rolnik, 2007)[4] or so called "resonant" communication occupying this interval as conceived by the Japanese.

Artistic revolutions in dance, notably American post-modernist and Japanese-Butoh (abbreviation *of Ankoku Butoh or "la danse des ténèbres" (in french)*[5]), rebelled against the institution. It was essential to question all choreographic referents, especially the time-space relation as well as the subjects of structure, relationship and organization. These revolutions have also questioned phenomena such as "presence", "conscience" and "reality". Throughout these periods, several body aesthetics emerged: let us recall

> the rebel body (Duncan), the barbaric body (Nijinski), the mystic body (St-Denis), the dynamic body (Humphrey), the chtonian body (Wigman), the pulsating body (Graham), the articulated body (Cunningham), the tactile body (Paxton), and the fluid body (Brown) (Boisclair, 2007 quoted in Crémézie, 1997)[6].

This tendency to use the dominant quality of the body as an instrument of representation is frequent in art and, according to Christine Palmiéri (Boisclair, 2007 quoted in Palmiéri, 1997), 'becomes an intersubjective space for moving identity exchanges, transforming itself through the layers of a collective fable'[7].

In light of this research regarding the interval, the fluid and tactile bodies are the ones that particularly interest us. We would add to that two other types of body aesthetics: the introspective body (Butoh), of which the recent work of dancer Hideyuki Yano (1943-1988) is a witness, and the collective body (Lygia Clark - Brazil). According to cultural critic Louise Boisclair (2007), our personal research seems to develop another kind of dance aesthetic: being "the trans(e)dance", an expression of her own invention, comprised of the combination of trance, or *trans (*recalling the trans-disciplinarity of our research and corporeal work), dance and (e) for energy, electronic, elasticity and electricity.

This 'Collective or Embryonic Body' - as named in the beginning of the process - we are developing is of the resonant collective genre, using somatic practice strategies in order to make room to for the renewing of proprioception and exteroception. It is interested in the existing potentiality of the collective body and integrates some of the strategies used by Paxton's tactile body, Brown's fluid body and Butoh's introspective body. According to Louise Boisclair, one must understand this

> larval body [original word "larvaire" in french] in terms of "embryonic body". This qualifier does not refer to individual dancing bodies, which are more energetic and malleable; rather, it defines this enlarged sonorous body, in a new born state, inchoate, unfinished, always looking to develop and balance itself out. This embryonic body, creature from an enlarged sonorous body, represents a state of fluid gestation in perpetual movement...[8] (Boisclair, 2007).

For Boisclair,

> the spectator internalizes the work, experiencing a full loss of bearings, in a mental and corporeal space enlarged by this capture." Technologies, used in such a way, would facilitate "the apparition of a physical as well as digital creature, visual and sonorous, a collective body composed of individual bodies connected as an enlarged sonorous body, as if the whole was becoming the reflection of invisible exchanges between human beings inside the intimacy of physical, energetic, kinetic bodies on one side, and digital and sonorous on the other side[9] (Boisclair, 2007).

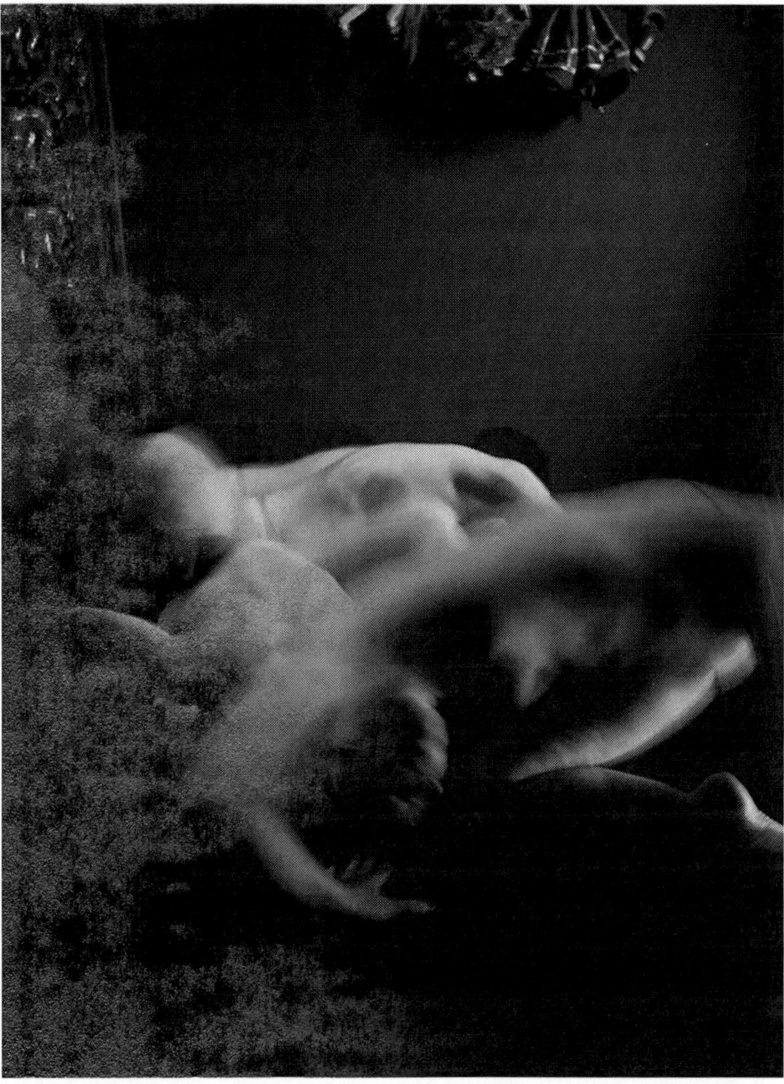

Fig.1 Images Meat Paradoxe / creators : Isabelle Choinière and Dominique Besson
Photos: Jean-François Gratton / Shoot Studio Montreal 2008

It is interesting to understand how Trisha Brown has constructed her fluid body. In fact, she works on the beginning and the end of the movement in dance. Influenced by the machine of the industrial period, she reflects on the notion of series and withdraws every transition between movements

> The temporal logic is disturbed: the beginning of a movement of a body part takes over from a former unfinished one … This game about the unfinished, the relieving and deviation creates a surprise effect which constantly restarts the movement…. The choreographer creates a movement that she herself qualifies as multidirectional…. (Fontaine, 2004)[10].

For Guy Scarpetta (Fontaine, 2004 quoted in Scarpetta, 1992), it is a body irredeemably 'transitory'[11]. For Geisha Fontaine, 'it installs another configuration.'[12] Steve Paxton, inventor of the contact dance and of the 'tactile body', is an improviser who 'uses tactile, kinaesthetic and proprioceptive sensations as bearings rather than the repeated and memorized movement, or points in space that are fixed' (Boucher, 2005).

The counter-culture of the sixties pushes dancers such as Paxton and Brown towards other types of training. 'Alexander, Bartenieff, Body-mind Centering, Feldenkrais, Trager somatic practices as well as martial arts reveal a new consciousness of posture, movement and body moving in relation with gravity and space.' (Boucher, 2005) Applied, these techniques develop fluidity of movement, body consciousness and stress elimination. Integrated, they question the 'Interval'.

Through dancer Hideyuki Yano's contemporary work on Butoh, the introspective body of this form of dance develops a very interesting relationship with the notion of interval. To Yano, 'past, present and future being one, time flows in every direction. … Since distance is interval, it is simultaneously spatial and temporal: one can move it, project it into the past or the future'[13] (Yano, 1983 quoted in Fontaine, 2004). Thus, for him, memory isn't a necessity anymore since the past is here.

This working method creates new circuits between corporeal and psychic memory, between experience and conscience.

For Yano, when choreography surpasses geometric and chronometric operations, 'it reaches the poetic soldered joint of time and space. It is like Japanese calligraphy which displays, by the blackness of the ink, the paper itself on which it must, in the single sweep of the brush, reveal a thousand of other possible sweeps'[14](Yano, [without date] quoted in Fontaine, 2004). This way of weaving the creative gesture has much in common with the different levels of revelation that technology, as referred to in the present context, can display.

4. The sonorous collective body: a connective and integrative learning strategy

We will introduce the somatic practices via the exteroception created by the new technologies we use. In other words, how exteroception renews our sensorial and perceptual experience. Somatic practices are centered on being conscious of the body in motion. They are about learning about the process of synergistic interactions between consciousness, movement and the environment. They are the experiential study of corporality.

In our research, the collective body represents the orgiastic figure, essential for the dissolution of the psycho-corporeal barrier; thus, the notion of non-docility and of loss of bearings, of control that we are developing through this reference to the orgiastic. From our point of view, it is a risky experiment. The orgiastic also speaks of the loss of compartmentalization of the body and of the senses and, accordingly, of another organization of body and senses and, eventually, of its structure and design. Therefore the sexual aspect – the part involving the physical body, its place and role – will also be deconstructed. Hans Bellmer with his 'dolls' and with his drawing called 'Céphalopode, années quarante, dessin au crayon', is a good example of deconstructed representation and was an inspiration for us.

The Collective Body is a self-organizing state: the body self-reorganizes through sensation itself. Here are some images (fig.2) showing a choreographic application of this deconstruction of the hierarchy of the body:

What makes taking this direction interesting is the fact that it leads to altered states. This altered state constitutes a loss of bearings. The Collective Body is a means to reach this second state.

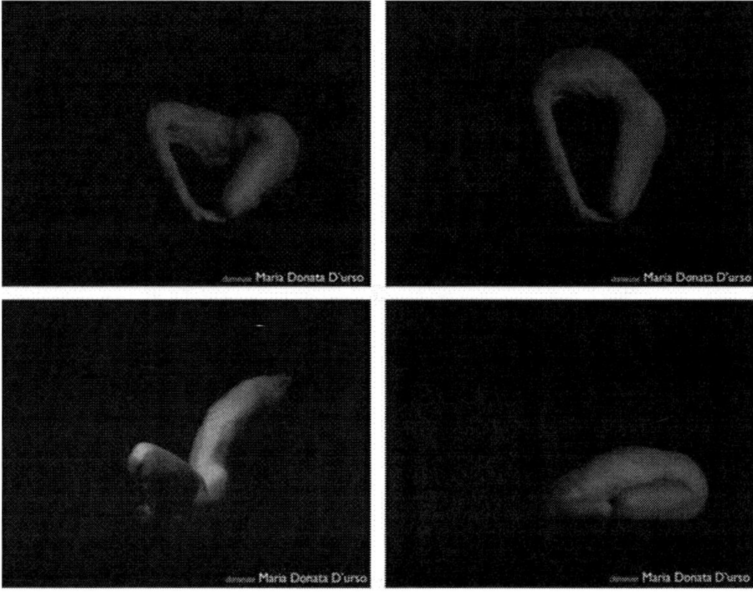

Fig. 2 Maria Donata D'urso. Creation : Pezzo O (due)

According to Laban (2007) in *La Maîtrise du mouvement*, and Michel Bernard (2001) in *De La création chorégraphique*, dance is an organization of the movement by the dance itself; these authors speak of the intelligence of the body. Dance is thus subjective and affective. This definition of dance and of *dance-ality*[15] (Bernard, 2001) has re-channeled our interest in pure sensation and senses, and has also organized an experience about revisiting the hierarchy of the body. Our work speaks of taking a distance from the code; it aims at de-structuring corporeal codes. It is a reasoned disturbing of all senses, of eroticism vectoring the body. According to Lacan, the body is covered by language. The body is 'normalized', the code is written into the body. The orgiastic goes further than the code, because it breaks the hierarchy. It is a non-linguistic state, a different organization of the senses.

It is at this point that Giacomo Rizzolatti's researches on mirror neuron systems seem of interest, because they bring forth an explanation about this "intelligence of the body" and the non-linguistic state we refer to. It is this non-linguistic state that is called upon to transmit knowledge from one dancer's body to the next. It is also a neuroscientific theory which takes over from Suely Rolnik's psychoanalytical one; it would explain, at least in part, this space of "vibratory" recognition and influence that leads to states of learning and transformation, even from a distance.

> The present findings strongly suggest that coding the intention associated with the actions of others is based on the activation of a neuronal chain formed by mirror neurons coding the observed motor act and by "logically related" mirror neurons coding the motor acts that are most likely to follow the observed one, in a given context. To ascribe an intention is to infer a forthcoming new goal, and this is an operation that the motor system does automatically[16] (Rizzolatti, 2005).

During the last phase of our experimentation in Spring 2008, we experimented with a creative process that is even more de-compartmentalized. Our goal was to create an 'evolutionary' content that would lead us to re-experience role sharing while creating the Sonorous Collective Body. The composer, by enlarging the concept of sonorous body, found herself playing the complementary part of user-generator. Two systems were used together (Fig. 3). The technological devices used to achieve this result remain largely invisible. The first device is a wireless microphone system for each of the dancers, hidden beneath black turbans they wear. The second device is the "Ring", an original computer programme created by the work's composer Dominique Besson with Olivier Koechlin and Antoine Schmitt designed to spatialize sound (Fig.4). Dominique Besson is a soundspace specialist. The spatialization tool called the Ring is a real time instrument used for spatial composition. It enables its user to drive, in public, sound sources detected on the stage or pre-recorded in the studio.

We have been able to observe that this 'symbiotic' sharing of the collective body leads to an extension of the proprioceptive as well as the exteroceptive relationship, while at the same time participating in the enrichment of an experiential corporeality. Of course, this result was achieved only because of the nature of the composer's artistic participation. Her experience as a musician (through her breath and the complexity of her pianist's touch) lead her to involve herself at the levels of supra-sensitive (concept similar to Brazilian artist Helio Oiticica's Supra-Sensorial[17]) and hyper-intimate, in the reality as much as mediated level.

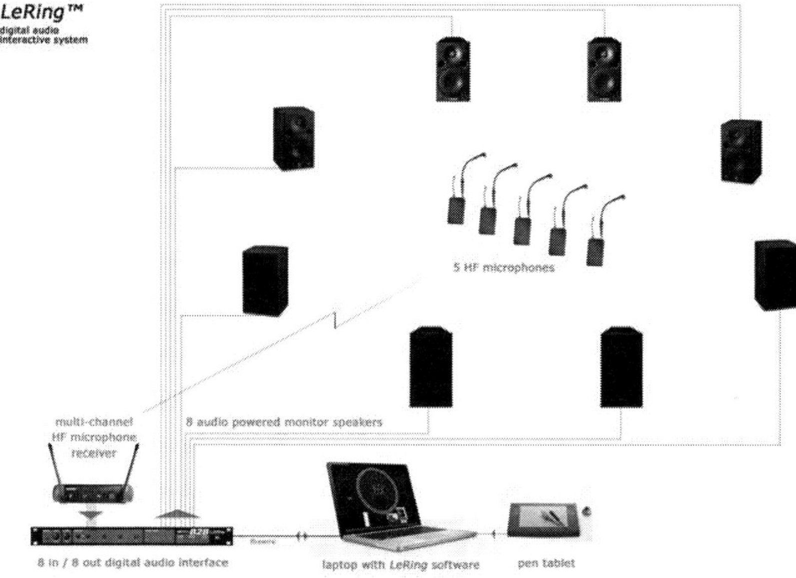

Fig.3

The event of these *real and mediated new relational dynamics* has modified the psycho-corporal state of both composer and dancers. We could feel the existence of a mutual influence in this process. Used for our new developments, the Ring follows

> the direction of an open system for real time spatialization equipped with functions of gradual memorization of the signal and trajectories. Being thus interfaced as real time data inside the Ring, the five sound sources generated by the dancers can be driven through space and time…Today it is possible to observe sound matter, to project it through physical space, to manipulate its components; in a word, to organize it (Fig.5). This new driveability reintroduces movement inside the compositional practice and makes it possible to observe the birth of new forms, intelligible but not always foreseeable (Fig. 6) [18] (Besson, 2009).

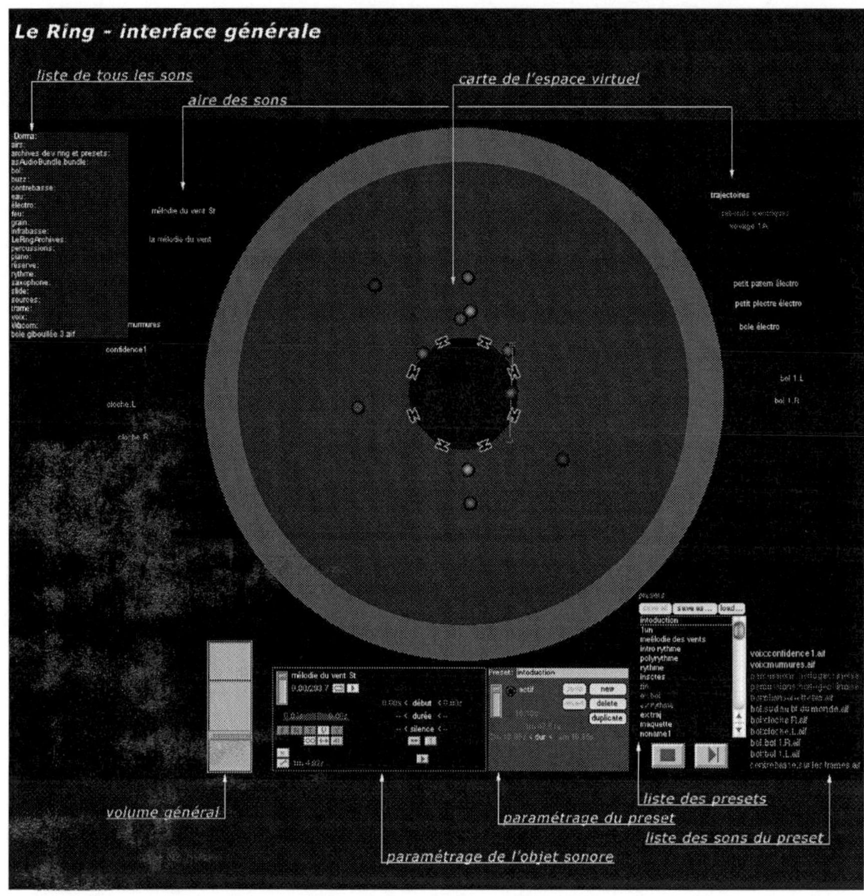

Fig.4, Composer Dominique Besson with Olivier Koechlin and Antoine Schmit, *Ring dispositif*, 2007.

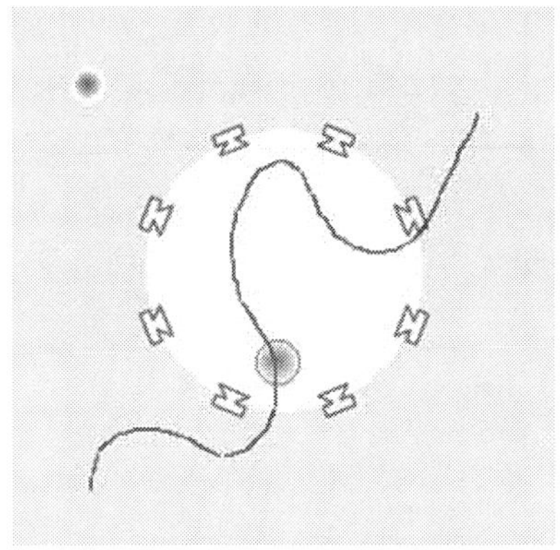

Fig.5

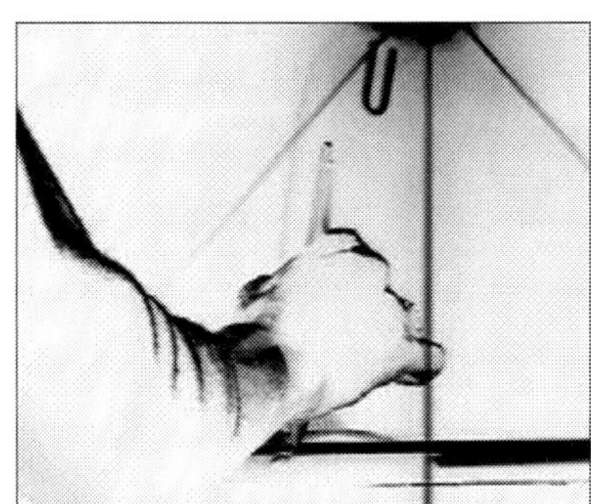

Fig.6

By asking the dancers to control their breath and by taking into account new relational parameters obtained by a kinaesthesia and a proprioception inherent to the dynamics of the Collective Body as a whole, we introduce 'a change of bearings by making something very intimate solid through sound: the inside perception of the movement' (Besson, 2009). In order to achieve musical results of a symbiotic magnitude, Dominique Besson reintroduces movement into the compositional practice through,

> (...) types of sound objects that, once animated with a life of their own in their spatiotemporal reiteration, form the sound space. In other words, it means organizing a time that opens and reveals the body. By letting the collective body go at its own pace towards creating the sound object, we open a form. Regarding the sound object, their exchange enables one to observe the birth of new forms that are constantly renewed, but circumstantialized.... Thus, we obtain a polymorphic and changing sound object characterized by a certain elasticity and which regulates itself like a body. Its projection inside physical space, its bursting forth from the circle of eight speakers acts in return on the proprioception of the dancers, involving an awareness of what is being created collectively. (Besson, 2009).

We think that this approach enables us to enrich the potential of the experience of corporeality rather than being stuck inside the causal process. The composer expresses this idea in a very touching way in the following words:

> In this fashion, we obtain a kind of moving form, animated, living, self organizing in an organic way: a sonorous body.' ... 'In such a situation,

> we must learn how to read movement by going around the limits of the perception of simultaneous phenomenon, how to get our bearings inside the space of the choreographic figure so we can reinterpret it by molding it inside the acoustic space by projecting, enlarging it …The collective body is very sensitive and reactive to its sonorous body, as if it would inhabit it, extend itself in it, discovering its length, its infinity. There is something here akin to flux, to sap rising, spreading or colliding … It is necessary to be able to decompose every choreographic figure … live them from the inside, in order to identify in a muscular way to the object of the research so as to optimize the spatial movement during performances. The composer becomes, in this context, the interpreter of the collective body. The relationship that develops among the dancers is intimate, almost affective. … The particularity of this writing is that its time is shared, dictated by the body and that things never reproduce identically… this experience once more feeds our imaginary by opening new horizons to us (Besson, 2009).

5. Conclusion

It takes time for changes in proprioceptive modes to occur and it also takes time to understand and assimilate the exteroceptive effect of technology on perceptual and sensorial modalities, and, in our case, to understand the transformation that is taking place. It is also important to review the different modes of production and kind of research necessary if one really aims to address the questions of meaning, aesthetics and corporality in these times of change that may be unsettling, but which are often rich in inspiration, in revelations ...

References

Ascott, R. (2006) 'Syncretic Reality ; new media in the technoetic culture'. Paper presented in the Conference : *Toward a Science of Consciousness*. Tucson, Arizona, U.S.A.

Banes, S. (1985) 'Festival International de Nouvelle Danse ; Montréal 1985, 19 au 29 septembre', Montreal : *Edition Parachute*. p. 52

—. (2002) *Terpsichore en baskets ; post-modern dance*, Paris: Edition Chiron.

Bernard, M. (2001) *De la création chorégraphique,* Pantin, France : Edition Centre national de la danse, Collection Recherches.

Besson, D. (2009) 'Le corps sonore, entre écriture chorégraphique et écriture musicale'. Paper Presented at the *Journée d'informatique Musicale – JIM'09. April 1-3, 2009*. Grenoble, France.

Blay, M. (2006) *Dictionnaire des concepts philosophiques,* Paris : Larousse CNRS Editions.

Boisclair, L. (2007), 'Isabelle Choinière de Corps Indice ; Autour des Demoiselles d'Avignon', Québec: in *Inter, art actuel, 'Espaces Sonore'*, No. 98 (winter).

Boucher, M. (2005), La danse, ses contextes et ses récits. Obtained Throught the Internet:
http://www.tangente.qc.ca/websichore/fra/DCR.htm,
[accessed 16/6/2008].

Crémézie, S. (1997) *La signature de la danse contemporaine*, Paris : Edition Chiron.

Cole, J., Dupras, N., Gallagher, S. (2000) 'Unity and Disunity in bodily awareness : phenomenology and neuroscience'. Paper presented at Conference ASSC4. Juin 29-July 2, 2000. Bruxelles, Belgium

de Kerckhove, D.(to be published in 2010) *Point of Being*, Italie, to be published in 2010.

Dempster, E. (1998) 'Women Writing the Body : Let's Watch a Little How She Dances', Londres : Routledge : in Alexandra Carter (dir), *The Routledge Dance Studies reader.*

Fontaine, G. (2004) *Les danses du temps ; Recherches sur la notion de temps en danse contemporaine*, Pantin, France: Edition Centre national de la danse, collection Recherches.

Ginsburg, C. (2006) *Le Mouvement et l'esprit ; une critique en forme d'essai,* Bruxelles, Belgique : Nouvelles de Danse No. 53 Scientifiquement Danse ; Quand la danse puise aux sciences et réciproquement.

Gunji, M. (1985) 'L'esthétique de la danse japonaise' , Paris: *Alternatives théâtrales*, No.22-23, April-May 1985.

Laban, R. V. (2007) *La maîtrise du mouvement* France : Ed. Acte sud.

Palmiéri, C. (2005) 'Le corps écranique : Figure du sensible et lieu de partage'.*Paper Presented at* the 73e Congress of the ACFAS. 2005. Chicoutimi, Québec. Obtained Throught the Internet: www.acfas.ca. [accessed 18/6/2008].

Rolnik, S. L'hybride de Lygia Clark. Obtained Throught the Internet: http://caosmose.net/suelyrolnik/textos.htm, [accessed 22/5/2007].

—. Figures nouvelles du Chaos ; les mutations de la subjectivité contemporaine. Obtained Throught the Internet:

http://caosmose.net/suelyrolnik/textos.htm [accessed 22/5/2007].
Weissberg, J.-L. (1988) *Paysages Virtuels ; image video, image de synthèse*, France: Editions Dis Voir, Series Prise de vue, Collection directed byDanièle Rivière.
Yano, H. (1983) 'Dérapage', Paris: *Théâtre/Public*, No.52-53, July 1983.
Yano, Hideyuki, 'Press pack of the performance' *Rivière Sumida*.

Reference without authors

Obtained Throught the Internet:
www.schenk.chore.art.free.fr/danse-buto-definition.htm, [accessed 18/6/2008].
Obtained Throught the Internet:
http://www.alexandertechnique-montreal.com/alexander_f.html, [accessed 18/6/2007].
Obtained Throught the Internet:
http://www.limsonline.org/lma_bf.html, [accessed 18/6/2007].
Obtained Throught the Internet:
http://www.bodymindcentering.com/About/AboutBMC/, [accessed 18/6/2007].
Obtained Throught the Internet:
http://www.enotes.com/alternative-medicine-encyclopedia/feldenkrais, [accessed 18/6/2007].
Obtained Throught the Internet:
http://www.answers.com/topic/trager-psychophysical-integration-1?cat=health, [accessed 18/6/2008].

Notes

[1] From the Greek *Sunaisthêsis*: "simultaneous perception": Plurality of sensory perception characterized by the perception of a supplementary perception to what is normally perceived by another part of the body or which involves another sensory domain.

[2] There are two types of perception: proprioception, through which we perceive what comes from the inside, and exteroception, or the perception of what comes from the outside. The Feldenkrais method is the study of proprioception that provides us with the invariables of our personal movements and the space that we incorporate: i.e. what he call our inner environment. The Feldenkrais method is part of the somatic practices in contemporary dance. Somatic practices are centred on developing an awareness of the moving body. These practices consist of learning synergistic interaction processes between consciousnes, movement and

the environment. They make up the experiential study of corporeality (ex : Alexander, Bartenieff, Body-Mind Centering, Feldenkrais, Pilates, etc.) Ginsburg, C. (2006) *Le Mouvement et l'esprit ; une critique en forme d'essai,* Bruxelles, Belgique : Nouvelles de Danse No. 53 Scientifiquement Danse; Quand la danse puise aux sciences et réciproquement. p.38.

[3] The Japanese word Mâ signifies space-time, and particularly the interval of time or space between an attitude and the next, an artistic transport of space-time.
Gunji, M. (1985) 'L'esthétique de la danse japonaise', Paris: *Alternatives théâtrales*, No.22-23, April-May 1985, p.12.

[4] Suely discusses the vibratory body in these terms: «This vibratory body is sensitive to the movements of the flows of the universes which pass through it. A body-egg, in which unknown intensive states germinate, These states are brought about by the new composition of flows that wander here and there, doing and undoing — the cartographies which I have referred to above. At times the germination accumulates until the body can no longer express itself in its actual form. Anxiety mounts: the beast grumbles, stamps its feet and ends up being sacrificed; its form becomes its shroud. If we allow ourselves to be taken in, it is the beginning of another body that is born immediately after death. – that is the state of creation. »
Rolnik, S. L'hybride de Lygia Clark. Obtained Throught the Internet: http://caosmose.net/suelyrolnik/textos.htm, [accessed 22/5/2007].

[5] The «Butoh » is an overall term which encompasses the whole avant-garde of Dance born after the War, and breaks up simultaneously with classical Japanese theater-dance and what has been brought by the West. Banes, S. (2002) *Terpsichore en baskets ; post-modern dance*, Paris: Edition Chiron. p.43.

[6] Crémézie, S. (1997) *La signature de la danse contemporaine*, Paris : Edition Chiron. Pp. 138 ; p.28.

[7] Palmiéri, C. (2005) 'Le corps écranique : Figure du sensible et lieu de partage'.*Paper Presented at* the 73e Congress of the ACFAS. 2005. Chicoutimi, Québec. Obtained Throught the Internet: www.acfas.ca. [accessed 18/6/2008].

[8] Boisclair, L. (2007), 'Isabelle Choinière de Corps Indice ; Autour des Demoiselles d'Avignon', Québec: in *Inter, art actuel, 'Espaces Sonore'*, No. 98 (winter), pp. 52-56.

[9] Idem.

[10] Fontaine, G. (2004) *Les danses du temps ; Recherches sur la notion de temps en danse contemporaine*, Pantin, France: Edition Centre national de la danse, collection Recherches.

[11] Dempster, E. (1998) 'Women Writing the Body : Let's Watch a Little How She Dances', Londres : Routledge : in Alexandra Carter (dir), *The Routledge Dance Studies reader.* pp.223-229.

[12] Idem. P.214.

[13] Yano, H. (1983) 'Dérapage', Paris: *Théâtre/Public*, No.52-53, July 1983. p.75.

[14] Yano, H. (1983) 'Dérapage', Paris: *Théâtre/Public*, No.52-53, July 1983. p. 74-76.

[15] *Dance-ality*, is a state of sensibility: a capacity to organize movement in an auto-affective and reflective way by the movement itself.

[16] Rizzolatti, G. (2005) 'Grasping the intentions of Others with One's Own Mirror Neuron System', USA: *PLoS Biology,* Vol. 3, Issue 3, e79. March 2005. p.0005.

[17] "Brazilian artist Helio Oiticica speaks of this phenomenon in his practice and explains how samba practice has helped him to develop his ideas on the Supra-Sensorial.

The Supra-Sensorial, promotes the expansion of the individual's normal sensory capacities in order to discover his/her internal creative center. The Supra-Sensorial could be represented by hallucinogenic states (induced with or without the use of drugs), religious trance and other alternate states of consciousness such as ecstasy and delirium facilitated by samba dance. For Oiticica, the Supra-sensorial created a complete de-aesthetization of art underscoring transformative processes... For Oiticica, samba was a conduit for the flow of energy and desire. Samba was a relay, a connector...he was incorporating in this process the kinetic knowledge of the body. Osthoff , S. (Updated 23 November 2004) '*Lygia Clark and Hélio Oiticica: A Legacy of Interactivity and Participation for a Telematic Future', Leonardo On-line*. p.8. Obtained Throught the Internet:
http://mitpress2.mit.edu/ejournals/Leonardo/isast/spec.projects/osthoff/osthoff.htm [accessed 22/5/2007].

[18] Besson, D. (2009) 'Le corps sonore, entre écriture chorégraphique et écriture musicale'. Paper Presented at the *Journée d'informatique Musicale – JIM'09. April 1-3, 2009.* Grenoble, France.
http://acroe.imag.fr/jim09/index.php/descrip/conf/schedConf/actesDominiqueBesson/muse-dbesson@gmail.com/http://tqp.free.fr/bio_Dominique_Besson/

CHAPTER TWO

TRANSDISCIPLINARY RESEARCH BRIDGING COGNITIVE LINGUISTICS AND DIGITAL PERFORMANCE: FROM MULTIMODAL CORPORA TO CHOREOGRAPHIC KNOWLEDGE-BASES

CARLA MONTEZ FERNANDES
AND STEPHAN JÜRGENS

Foreword

This chapter presents the **Transmedia Knowledge Base project** (TKB), a transdisciplinary project coordinated by Carla Fernandes at CLUNL[1], lying in the interstices between cognitive linguistics, contemporary dance studies and the new media technologies, accommodating two other endeavours to develop user-centered interaction design in the realm of digital performance.

Building on practice-based research collaborations with choreographers Rui Horta in Portugal, Emio Greco in Amsterdam (in the framework of the international project *Inside Movement Knowledge*[2]) and Lisbon-based choreographer Stephan Jürgens (with his digital performance **.txt**), the authors try to integrate the three idiosyncratic but closely-related perspectives into a common frame, thus hoping to enhance the development of interactive knowledge bases sharing similar conceptual structures.

An interactive multimodal glossary designed by Carla Fernandes to accommodate Horta's conceptual structure in the TKB project, as well as a parallel hypertext glossary of Emio Greco's terms and definitions used to improve the code of his installation DS/DM (*Double Skin/Double Mind*) are currently being compiled.

Stephan Jürgens also has been developing an evolving web-based glossary for digital performance over the past few years, which consists of compositional concepts, technical principles and forms of collaboration. This glossary serves both as "translator" of the bodily knowledge of choreographers and performers, and as "generator" of new creative strategies for the collaborative design of interactive systems for live performance. An example of this methodology is presented in this paper, demonstrating the application of a compositional concept to explore the custom-built TKB video annotator in its condition of creation-tool in the choreographic process.

Introduction

The understanding, organization and transmission of the core concepts of a specific knowledge domain inevitably depends on a structured analysis of the discourses originated inside that domain.

Knowledge is organized in our memory under distinct domain headings; terminologies differ from domain to domain, which precisely is what allows metaphorical transfers, such as the ones occurring in interdisciplinary projects and their subsequently emergent "translation" processes.

Cognitively oriented discourse/semiotic analysis offers both theoretical insights and motivates representational requirements for the semantics of tools such as Emio Greco's *DS/DM* installation or the TKB's video annotator, based on Horta's interactive multimodal glossary, or the user-centred creation-tool we are developing for TKB as well.

The closely-related research projects presented in this paper, as examples of inter- and trans-disciplinarity practices, try to integrate methods and theories developed in the disciplines of contemporary choreography, linguistics, and new media art with methods and theories derived from cognitive science and semiotics, with the ultimate aim of providing new insights into the realm of human meaning production.

Creativity and innovation occur less and less within a discipline, but increasingly in the contact zone of various disciplines. New technologies are used especially to share knowledge that would otherwise be restricted to the happy few insiders, members of the domain specific communities in question.

By crossing different research methodologies, world perspectives and idiosyncratic intentions, thus allowing their productive inter-contamination, we wish to implement the fundamental trans-boundary circulation of ideas and implicit concepts, by starting to build the grounding pillars for a toll-free bridge between (only) apparently separated knowledge areas.

The potential of evolving glossaries in collaborative creative processes will be discussed regarding the creation of interactive knowledge databases, the reflection and analysis of the individual artistic creative process, and the generation of new creative strategies in the field of performative rich media environments.

Three endeavours to develop user-centered interaction design in the realm of digital performance will be described in the next sections, focusing both on their similarities and specificities and following an integration approach as much as possible.

1. The TKB project: A Transmedia Knowledge-Base

Correlated to the other two endeavours to be presented below, indeed currently functioning as an umbrella for both of them, the *TKB project* aims at the design and construction of an open-ended multimodal knowledge-base to dynamically document, structure, annotate and browse a range of recently created digital dance pieces. It offers above all a transdisciplinary university-based structure for reflection on original documentation models for contemporary choreography and performance.

The TKB research project[3] was designed and initiated by Carla Fernandes at CLUNL in 2008 as a follow-up of the previously gained experience with the semiotic micro-analysis of Rui Horta's piece *SetUp* [4] in the framework of a Post-Doctoral research project; it is currently running under her own coordination with the collaboration of several international research partners and consultants, namely: *Espaço do Tempo*[5] (Rui Horta's Choreographic Centre in Montemor-o-Novo); University of Amsterdam – AHK (with Bertha Bermudez and Scott DeLahunta); Ohio State University (Advanced Computing Center for the Arts and Design / Forsythe Foundation, with Norah Zuniga Shaw); *Universidade Nova de Lisboa*: Faculty of Social and Human Sciences (CLUNL - Linguistics

Centre, with Rute Costa, and INET-MD, with Stephan Jürgens); Faculty of Science and Technology (Interactive Multimedia Group - Department of Computer Science, with Nuno Correia); and *Universidade do Porto* (CLUP – Linguistics Centre, with Isabel Rodrigues).

It situates itself in a hybrid territory between cognitive linguistics, dance research and new media technologies and its initial motivation and start-up questions were the following:

- How is a choreographer's *imagetic* (not only verbal) type of thought translated into an embodied-type of *thought in motion* via the dancers?
- Can choreography be interpreted as thoughts in motion?
- What is the impact of verbal language on the dancers' movements?
- When does the dancing body demand words and vice-versa?

The global purpose of TKB, since its very beginning, has been to extend the scope and application of the "documentation" concept to contemporary dance in different ways by taking a closer look at the cognitive process of *choreographic thinking* and therefore hopefully contribute to the domains of multimodal corpora, terminological ontologies, cognition and verbal-nonverbal relations.

TKB's main aims include three complementary components, namely:

1 - Linguistic annotation;
2 – Custom-made software for annotation and motion analysis;
3 - Creation-oriented tool.

Component 1, *Linguistic annotation*, includes the following applications:

i) Video indexation and verbal annotation of multiple rehearsal videos;
ii) Creation of an idiosyncratic glossary to define the terms used;
iii) Prototype of online archive for Portuguese contemporary dance.

By using a custom-made video annotator, the aim of Component 1 has been to annotate and index original videos from dance performances, shot on site during their creation and rehearsal phases, in a first stage those corresponding to the piece *SetUp* by Rui Horta. *SetUp* was then contrasted with two other pieces by the same choreographer, with which it is considered to form a trilogy: *Pixel – SetUp – Scope.* SetUp has been the focus of a case study to be followed by the analysis of Stephan Jürgens' digital performance ***.txt*** during TKB's further developments, both for contrasting and evaluation purposes.

The methodology followed for Component 1 is the one underlying the linguistic annotation of textual *corpora* (in the same way as done for the *SetUp* case study while using the ANVIL video annotation tool), where digital videos instead of texts are parsed, in order to enable the analysis of movement sequences that may be tagged as the "minimal units" or *dancemes* (our suggestion) of each choreographer's "grammar".

The lexical annotation of video frames is based on the principles of the conceptual metaphor theory and its "embodiment" postulates (Johnson 1990). It has mainly been applied to:

a) the influence or direct effect of the use of speech in contemporary dance upon the more distinctive, recurrent or emblematic gestures, phrases or body movement sequences;
b) other choreographic elements such as the physical space (architectural structures), the multimedia resources, the lights design, the sound, or even the spectator's participation in the event. This initiative has led us to the development of the TKB itself in its present configuration: a transmedia knowledge base also in the sense that the several different modalities (verbal and non-verbal) are contaminating each other in such a way that it is not the aesthetic body anymore which is in the foreground of our analysis, but rather the interconnections of choreographic thought and human motion in the whole piece as a unit.

The motivation for the creation of an idiosyncratic glossary (Component 1. ii) to define the terms used by Rui Horta has derived from the need felt in the first place by each of the research teams involved to *come to terms* with the obviously different, culture-bound and case-specific terminology used by the choreographer in question. Moreover, we have soon realized that the iterative design of the TKB's interface and related digital archive would have to be closely articulated with the data contained in the verbal annotations. And this naturally implied that their structuring categories, principles or basic units should be defined as precisely as possible, in order to allow the retrieval and translatability of at least the more relevant or salient analytical features of a certain piece into the computational parameters needed for a more automatic motion recognition process in the near future.

In this sense, an interactive multimodal glossary is currently under development to be structured as a work-in-progress Knowledge-Base of choreographic elements used by Rui Horta and his interpreters; it is intended to be a rather flexible tool, in the sense that its underlying structure, inspired by the *Frame theory* (in its derivation from artificial intelligence applications to linguistics and lexicographical products), will be adapted to accommodate other choreographers' concepts and possible taxonomies as well, as is the case with our partner Bertha Bermudez working for the *DS/DM* hypertext glossary with Emio Greco|PC in Amsterdam.

Besides gathering, defining and ordering textual and visual data, the emphasis will be placed on the investigation, creation and design of a multimodal interactive user interface, where terms, definitions, descriptions, notations and live demonstrations will be available to the viewer through video, sound and icons.

Concerning the prototype for a Digital Archive (component 1. iii) of selected Portuguese contemporary dance creations, our mid-term aim is to gradually compile in the transmedia knowledge-base the newest creations of international choreographers showing interest in this initiative, as well as, in the longer run, to cover the existing resources documenting the choreographic productions of the last three decades in Portugal. The future digital archive should also include the press and television previously existing documentation, and a spectator's gallery for feed-back and audience intervention after a piece is premiered.

Component 2, the development of a *custom-made software tool for annotation* and motion analysis, includes the following modules:
i) A video annotator
ii) An Information & Knowledge Management
iii) A motion analysis research plug-in

Component 2 includes the development of a custom-made video annotator[6], an information & knowledge management system, as the interface to connect the three different modules involved, and a motion analysis research module. The latter should work as a plug-in module towards a multi-person semi-automatic system to analyze the human body motion in video dance sequences (cf. Guo 2006). According to Norman (2009:4), "exploitation of datasets of this complexity calls for novel index-based retrieval tools, where annotated data features can be identified in response to multiple, composite query criteria", which is exactly what we intend to experiment in this component.

The three mentioned modules of Component 2 will correspond to two different applications: one for annotation and another one, web-based, for content access and browsing.

Component 3, a *Creation-oriented tool*, includes the development of a tool for the choreographers' creation process and their personal archives.

The development of the prototype for a creation-oriented tool is to be based on the outcomes of the earlier stages of the TKB project, particularly on the results of the annotated video corpora and the possibilities provided by the software development with the aim of feeding back to the choreographic creative process.

A choreographer's creation process is evidently highly individual and specific, which is why the design of the video annotator as creation-tool will be approached from a combination of the practitioner and researcher's perspective. For the development of a first prototype, choreographer and researcher Stephan Jürgens was invited to collaborate on the design and to test the future web-based TKB interface with regard to his creative process and choreographic methods.

The interface is planned to provide different modes for different types of users, e.g., choreographers or archive users. One important way of using the TKB annotator is a user-led mode allowing a choreographer to annotate relevant information in real-time during rehearsal and performance; simultaneously the annotator can serve as an auxiliary tool for personal archiving intentions of the artist. Naturally this user-led mode provides more access privileges to the annotator than a user-centred mode, in which a researcher, for example, can browse existing annotations made by a given choreographer and authorized for public consultation; or the researcher might want to add his own comments as well. The difference between both modes is that the choreographer can customize the interface for his needs, whereas the archive user has much fewer access privileges.

The TKB annotator interface will be developed by a new media designer with the collaboration of Stephan Jürgens and Rui Horta[7]. Most of the annotator' specifications will be derived from the results of the manual video annotations[8], which in their turn will inform the future digital archive itself.

2. A Digital Performance Glossary applied to the *TKB creation-tool*

Over the past few years, Jürgens has been developing a constantly evolving glossary for digital performance, consisting of compositional concepts, technical principles and forms of collaboration. This glossary serves in part as "translator" of the bodily knowledge of choreographers and performers, and partly as "generator" of new creative strategies and the collaborative design of interactive systems for live performance. The glossary is planned to be made available online and further developed on the basis of user feedback and input. Its main principles can be employed to quickly and efficiently create the specific terminology used with the TKB annotator. For example, the concept of "**Development Cycle**" was applied to develop the research questions presented below for testing the TKB creation-tool. According to this principle, choreographic processes in the field of Digital Performance can be divided into two cycles consisting of the following phases:

Cycle one: creation of a work

1. Artistic concept: research and training (e.g. working with a new interactive system)
2. Creating material
3. Designing strategies for interaction
4. Developing micro- and macro-structures of the performance

Cycle two: iteration of the work

5. Public performance
6. Documentation of the work (rehearsal and performance)
7. Re-staging / re-creating a work

Phases 1-4 can be considered a first cycle (creation of a work) and phases 5-7 a second cycle (iteration of the work after creation). Phase 7 of the second cycle leads back into one or more phases of the first cycle.

Three tasks have been developed for the TKB creation-tool to address design creative strategies within specific phases of the Development Cycle:

Task 1 (first cycle, phases 2-3)

Choreographers working with interactive systems often experience difficulties in recording rehearsal sessions in a satisfactory way. While it is common practice to film the dancer's movement in rehearsal efficiently, it is often impossible to film the projected visual output of the interactive system simultaneously.

We are documenting rehearsals in which interactive systems with projected visual output are used, by means of the custom-built TKB video annotator, which provides the possibility to synchronize two or more video streams and annotate the choreographer's ideas, comments or sketches. In this way we can clearly visualize correlations between the dancers' movement and the visual output of the interactive system.

Task 2 (first cycle, phase 4)

In the 80s and 90s *mapping* approaches were prevalent to define the relation between sensory input and multimedia output of an interactive system. During the past years attempts have been made to improve the "intelligence" of interactive systems, for example to develop computational forms of perception and interpretation of the input as a base for adequate output (Bevilacqua et al. 2007; Downie 2005; Camurri et al. 2005).

For this second task we have developed a glossary for Stephan Jürgens' digital solo performance **.txt** (2007-09). Subsequently it will be tested how this glossary can help to improve the programming of two specifically selected scenes of this work. In other words, we will examine how to use this particular glossary in combination with the parameters of the motion analysis module of the TKB interface, in order to program a more autonomous yet meaningful media output of the interactive system.

Task 3 (second cycle)

Finally, we will focus on the potential of the TKB interface for re-staging a digital performance, which corresponds to the second development cycle. A group of dancers with diverse training backgrounds will work on re-staging selected scenes from the **.txt** project. The goal here is to compare how the different dancers make use of the existing annotations to learn and perform the solo. A further research question here is whether the manual annotations can successfully communicate the choreographer's intentions; and to what extent the dancers should use the annotation tools themselves.

3. The DS/DM glossary[9]

Dance Company Emio Greco | PC (ICKamsterdam) and the research group Art Practice and Development (Amsterdam School of the Arts) have established a partnership with Carla Fernandes aiming at joint work methods and outcomes within the TKB project, mainly regarding linguistic-related issues, such as the organization of terminological data into interactive knowledge-bases.

Since the beginning of their artistic work, dance company Emio Greco | PC has focused on an internal reflection of their artistic praxis. This reflection has lead to the development of different activities within the field of art practice based research, dance education and dance discourse. Through their interdisciplinary research project *Inside Movement Knowledge* (started Septembre 2008 in Amsterdam), questions around dance transmission, documentation models, dance notation and recreation have been confronted with different disciplines like dance notation, cognitive linguistics and new media design. In the framework of Bertha Bermudez's partnership with TKB, part of this research project is also to create a hypertextual glossary, under Fernandes' guidance, due to represent the cognitive schema of the artistic work produced since 1995 by Emio Greco and Pieter C. Scholten.

The Emio Greco | PC generic glossary aims to reveal and define the terminology used among their creative process, as well as to investigate new trends on issues of interaction and dance documentation. The glossary project has departed from a first draft of the *Double Skin /Double Mind* workshop glossary, created as a tool of communication between the different disciplines involved within the *IMK* project. Throughout three years, the original draft of terms will be complemented with concepts relating to the *basic principles* of the work (contextual concepts that help understand the main philosophical and creative ideas of the choreographers), *creative structures* like pre-choreographic elements, phrases and overall performance structures and concepts revealed in the choreographers' discourse.

Conclusions and further developments

Common to the three projects described above, each of them involving interactive online glossaries or knowledge-bases, is their implicit user-centred approach. Furthermore, all these glossaries in progress have been designed according (and are oriented) to two different types of end-users: those having access to the respective glossaries' "back-offices" and those not having access to them. In other words, once each glossary annotation grid has been stabilized, with categories, types, principles or minimal units to be indexed and annotated in their respective tracks, only the researchers and the choreographers involved in the whole process will have access to the main programming frames of the glossaries. The external end-users, such as any dance student, scholar or the general audience of a particular choreographer, will not be able to change the original semantic grid or frame, although they are strongly encouraged to make comments to all the categories and tracks previously annotated. To give just one example, Rui Horta's broad knowledge-base will include a public-dedicated gallery, where a world-open space should work as the beginning of an original and democratic database of audience responses/criticism to the annotated performances available in the digital archive. To summarize, while each choreographer and respective research team can (and are meant to!) customize their own annotations' *slots* and *fillers*, the external users can only add their comments to the already existing annotation tracks. *Slots* cannot be altered, since their customization requires a complete re-programming of the conceptual frame as a coherent whole.

Through the development of the three parallel endeavours described in this paper, Rui Horta, Emio Greco | PC, Stephan Jürgens, and their respective researcher teams, aim to provide the broader public with further understanding of their unique individual universes, and ultimately a deeper insight into the dance creative praxis in general.

In conclusion, it seems that, at the present, several perspectives on the use of ICT technologies in general, and the need for project-specific cross-disciplinary terminology in particular have greatly benefited from the analysis of digitized dance video and motion tracking/capture data (Lansdale et al. 2003; Norman. 2006). Publications on the development and use of glossaries and *lexica* evolving during the creative process

(Shaw and Lewis, 2006) are very few. We hope to contribute with the TKB creation-tool to show how, based on such specific glossaries, intuitive programming possibilities can be provided for artists in the realm of digital performance, empowering them to design new creative strategies for their particular artistic processes.

The potential of evolving glossaries in collaborative creative processes has been discussed regarding the creation of interactive knowledge-bases, the reflection and analysis of the individual artistic creative process and the generation of new creative strategies in the field of performative rich media environments.

TKB's web-based broader application is scheduled to be launched by 2012, with both its theoretical and practice-based results being especially relevant for the dance-related structures in Portugal, higher education schools for contemporary dance and choreography, contemporary art museums and, more specifically, for knowledge building inside the scientific communities of linguistics, cognition, multimodal corpora and new media technologies. Its final outputs should include the creation from scratch of a new customized video annotator, the iterative design of all the TKB's software applications, a prototype for an interactive digital archive and a motion capture plug-in for applied research. Future developments should include the production of compressed video visualizations of body motion in dance and the use of neurology's imaging technology (fMRI) over the involved choreographers and dancers' mental spaces after a piece has been performed.

References

Bevilacqua, F., Guédy, F., Schnell, N., Fléty, E. & Leroy, N. (2007) Wireless sensor interface and gesture-follower for music pedagogy. *2007 Conference on New Interfaces for Musical Expression (NIME07).* New York.

Brandt,P.A. 2005. Spaces, Domains, and Meaning. Essays in Cognitive Semiotics. Bern: Peter Lang Verlag.

Camurri, A., De Poli, G., Friberg, A., Leman, M. & Volpe, G. (2005) The MEGA Project: Analysis and Synthesis of Multisensory Expressive Gesture in Performing Art Applications. *Journal of New Music Research,* 34, 5 - 21, November 04, 2008.

Correia, N. et al. 2002. Annotations as multiple perspectives of video content. In Proceedings of the 10th ACM international conference on

Multimedia. ACM MULTIMEDIA´02. ACM Press, New York, NY, 283-286.

DeLahunta,S. 2006. ConstructingMemories in http://tkbproject.files.wordpress.com/2009/01/scottdelahunta_2006_constructing-memories.pdf

Downie, M. (2005) Choreographing the extended agent : performance graphics for dance theater. *Massachusetts Institute of Technology. Dept. of Architecture. Program In Media Arts and Sciences.*

Fernandes, C. & Costa, R. 2008. "Indexação vídeo e anotação linguística de criações coreográficas contemporâneas: para uma ontologia multimédia" in Estudos Linguísticos / Linguistic Studies, Edições Colibri: Lisboa, pp. 11-18. http://tkbproject.files.wordpress.com/2009/01/carlafernandes_linguistic-studies-journal.pdf

Fernandes, C. & Costa, R. 2009 (forthcoming). "Looking for the linguistic knowledge behind the curtains of contemporary dance: the case of Rui Horta's creative process" in *Art, Brain and Language*. Special Issue of *International Journal of Arts and Technology*. Inderscience Publishers.

Guo, F. & Qian, G. 2006. Dance Posture Recognition Using Wide-baseline Orthogonal Stereo Cameras. In Proceedings of the 7th international Conference on Automatic Face and Gesture Recognition (April 10 - 12, 2006). FGR. IEEE Computer Society, Washington, DC, 481-486.

Jesus, R., Abrantes, A., Correia, N. 2006. Photo Retrieval from Personal Memories using Generic Concepts. Advances in Multimedia Information Processing - PCM, Springer LNCS, 2006. 4261: p. 633-640.

Johnson, M. 1990. *The body in the mind.* Chicago: Chicago University Press.

Jürgens. S. 2008. "Expanding Choreographic Resources: Generative Techniques in Contemporary Life Performance and New Media Art" in: Tércio, Daniel (ed.) TeDance - Perspectives on Technologically Expanded Dance, Lisbon, Faculdade Motricidade Humana/Technical University of Lisbon.

Kipp, M. 2008. "Spatiotemporal Coding in ANVIL" In: Proceedings of the 6th international conference on Language Resources and Evaluation (LREC-08).

Lansdale, J., Deveril, Carr, L., Hall, W. & Miles-Board, T. (2003) Decentering the dancing text: from dance intertext to hypertext. *Proceedings of the fourteenth ACM conference on Hypertext and hypermedia 1-58113-704-4.* Nottingham, UK, ACM.

Lakoff & Johnson, 1999. *Philosophy in the Flesh: The embodied Mind and its challenge to Western Thought*. New York: Basic Books.
Norman, S. J. 2006. Generic Versus Idiosyncratic Expression in Live Performance Using Digital Tools. *Performance Research,* 11, 23 - 29
Norman, S. J. et al. 2009. AMUC Research Report – Associated Motion capture User Categories. Culture Lab: Newcastle.
Shaw, N. Z. & LEWIS, M. (2006) Inflecting Particles: Locating generative indexes for performance in the interstices of dance and computer science. *Performance Research,* 11, 75 - 86

Notes

[1] http://www.clunl.edu.pt/PT/projecto.asp?id=1555&mid=138

[2] *Inside Movement Knowledge* (IMK) is an interdisciplinary research project, which involves researchers from the Netherlands Media Institute, the Amsterdam School for the Arts, the Theatre & Dance Studies Department at Utrecht University, and a group of international collaborators, where Carla Fernandes is included.

[3] The TKB Project has been approved for national funding in August 2009.

[4] A practice-based research case-study described in Fernandes & Costa 2009 (in print). "Looking for the linguistic knowledge behind the curtains of contemporary dance: the case of Rui Horta's creative process" in *Art, Bain and Language*, Special Issue of *International Journal of Arts and Technology*. Inderscience Publishers.

[5] http://www.oespacodotempo.pt/en/prog.php?idpan=pro_det&recid=477

[6] The research partners responsible for this module (from the *Interactive Multimedia Group* at FCT/UNL) have previously developed algorithms for image and video annotation that will be generalized in the scope of the TKB project. It is a framework for the identification of semantic events that can be tailored for a specific application, combining low level image processing with classification mechanisms in order to annotate images or videos.

[7] We also count on a contemporary dance-expert consultant, Maria José Fazenda, a dance anthropologist at Lisbon's Higher Education School for Dance, and a facilitator consultant for the project's knowledge circulation, Scott DeLahunta, Writing Research Associates, Amsterdam.

[8] We hope to be contributing for pioneering ways of processing this type of manually annotated data and are aware that this will be an important challenge for our research group in the sense that usually (and quoting Melissa Terras) "humanities data has a tendency to be fuzzy, heterogeneous, of varying quality, and transcribed by human researchers, making humanities data difficult (and different) to deal with computationally." In ReACH: Researching –Science Analysis of Census Holdings, AHRC Arts and Humanities e-Science Workshop Series, Project Report, http://www.ucl.ac.uk/reach/.

[9] This section has been adapted from a previous text by Bertha Bermudez in the framework of her partnership in the TKB project. Acknowledgements are due for her agreement to see it quoted here.

CHAPTER THREE

"THE MUSIC ONE PARTICIPATES IN"

KAZUHIRO JO AND ATAU TANAKA

1. Introduction

Content created by users is a public affair. In the cultural field of music, this includes diverse activities of listening, sharing, editing, recording. Jacques Attali predicts that music will become a network of *composition*, where people actively participate in music-as-process, as a form of collective play [Attali, 1985]. Christopher Small coined the term, *musicking*, to describe music as a social act [Small, 1998]. This sets a context of participation for acts of sound making practice - how can composers, authors, and artists conceive of new forms of music where the listener enters into the process of co-creation?

Barthes [Barthes, 1977] divides music into two categories: the music one listens to and the music one plays. The former occurs when people engage passively with sound representations through the act of listening. The latter occurs when people subjectively engage in the creation of sound where listening takes on a subordinate role. In recent sound making practice, the boundary between the two is becoming increasingly blurred. Here, we describe a body of musical work where people subjectively engage with sound representations through listening and simultaneously engage with the creation of sound. In these pieces, each person is a listener of others, and a performer to others. We describe this practice as "the music one participates in".

In such a dynamic of participatory creativity, traditional distinctions between musicians (composers, performers) and audiences, or, for that matter, between musicians and non-musicians become less clear. Conventional musical training and skills, while still useful, are no longer an absolute requirement: each participant, regardless of level of training, is able to produce something they could call and enjoy as "music". [Auslander, 2000]

Cooperation and collaborative musical experiences [Blaine and Fels, 2003] and interconnected musical networks [Weinberg, 2005] have been discussed mostly from the point of view of interactive technologies. Here, we focus on the human dimensions of participatory sound making practice. In this, we are not conclusive about the fastened role of people in music making. Our emphasis instead is on the boundary of the roles and the dynamics of participation.

We consider the meaning of participation by looking at various roles in sound making practice. While this includes familiar roles such as composer, conductor, or performer (i.e. artist), in contemporary sound making practice they have gradually shifted. We see a shift of focus from the listener as consumer, who once passively received sound representations to becoming an actor, or actant, actively involved in sound production.

2. Participation

Participation has been discussed in fields ranging from education through social science to contemporary art. Lave and Wenger view learning as situated activity [Lave and Wenger, 1991]. Drawing on examples of practice from apprenticeship systems they describe the process by which newcomers become part of a community of practice. They argue that the mastery of knowledge and skill requires newcomers to move toward full participation in the socio cultural practices of a community.

In the social sciences, Arnstein defines broad three levels of citizen participation: *non-participation*, *tokenism*, and *citizen power* within which are eight rungs (from *manipulation* to *citizen control*) [Arnstein, 1969].

> ... "non-participation" that have been contrived by some to substitute for genuine participation. Their real object is not to enable people to participate in planning or conducting programs, but to enable power holders to "educate" or "cure" the participants.
>
> ... "tokenism" allow the have-nots to hear and to have a voice. When they are proffered by power holders as the total extent of participation, citizens may indeed hear and be heard. But under these conditions they lack the power to … changing the status quo and retain for the power holders the right to decide,

> ... "citizen power" … increasing degrees of decision-making clout. ... enables participant to negotiate and engage in trade-offs with traditional power holders. ... have-not citizens obtain the majority of decision-making seats, or full managerial power.

In the area of contemporary art, Bishop describes the social dimension of participation in art practices that strive to collapse the distinction between performer and audience [Bishop, 2006]. She observes three motivating agendas: 1.) activation to create subjects who determine their own social and political reality in a work, 2.) authorship to cede control of a work entailing aesthetic benefits of greater risk and unpredictability, and 3.) community as the social bond through a collective elaboration of meaning.

3. Musical Participation

In order to map these sociological notions of participation to the open-ended potential of music noted by Attali, Barthes, and Small, the sustainability of musical communities and methods for encouraging participation become crucial. Here we adapt Arnstein's three levels of participation to explore different means of participation in sound making practice. We are interested in understanding and supporting how people engage socially with music. Instead of directly proposing new modes of musical production, we propose ways of looking at emergent creative situations that may lead to new forms of musical engagement.

We propose a matrix that maps Arnstein's levels of participation against four different perspectives of sound making practice. Drawing upon acoustics, computer music, and performance theory, we identify the perspectives: *sound*, *instrument*, *process*, and *performance*. We validate the matrix by using it to describe existing works from experimental music, contemporary art, and new media. We then apply the matrix to specific examples from our own sound-based artistic projects where participation was a fundamental element. By doing so, we hope to elucidate the boundary across artistic roles and the dynamics of participation.

3.1 Four perspectives of sound making practice

3.1.1 Sound

We begin by considering acoustics as a way of distinguishing sound making practice from music. Acoustic sound is defined as the coupling of resonating bodies in a fixed or dynamic relationship. With electronic sound, the relationship becomes decoupled – sound and the resonating body can be considered independently [Bongers, 2007]. As a definition of sound, we follow the notion of timbre, "the attribute of sensation in terms of which a listener can judge that two sounds similarly presented and having the same loudness and pitch are dissimilar" [ASA, 1960], and extend the notion from notation-based musical representation to naturally occurring aural phenomena. People articulate their expression of sounds through the control of parameters that include but are not limited to pitch, volume, spectral shaping, and timing.

3.1.2 Instrument

We distinguish the set of objects that people manipulate to produce sounds as musical instruments. The range of objects can be diverse, from acoustic instruments through electronic equipments, to recorded media. An instrument is able to change musical context and produce different kinds of music, at the same time similar sounds can be created from different instruments. How we choose to control instrumental parameters affects the perception and the playability of the instrument [Hunt et al, 2002]. We distinguish the idiosyncratic, expressive quality of instruments from the utilitarian quality of tools. A musical instrument is not meant to carry out a single defined task in the way that a tool is. Instead, a musical instrument is able to change context, withstanding changes of musical style played on it while maintaining its identity. What might be considered imperfections or limitations from the perspective of tool design often contribute to the personality of a musical instrument [Tanaka, 2009].

3.1.3 Process

We define the sequence of actions that people carry out during their participation as process. In the traditional classical orchestra, the composer's score provides indications for the performers. Process in this case is the execution by instrumentalists of notated representation of music written by a composer as indicated by a conductor. Likewise the process of music listening in a concert is the ritual of seating, listening, and expressing appreciation by applause. In other sound making practice, these procedures range widely from designing instructions for game-like processes [McClary, 1986] to reaction to and from the others in improvisation [Bailey, 1980].

3.1.4 Performance

Schechner defines performance as "an activity done by an individual or group in the presence of and for another individual or group" [Schechner

1988: 22]. We follow this and draw upon Goffman's notion of social performance [Goffman, 1959] to consider people's listening and participatory musical activities as dramaturgical interaction, and thus forms of performance.

The position and resonance of sound define acoustic fields of space. The parameters allowing manipulation of an instrument provide diverse forms of playability. The movement of other participants by process result in dynamic change of sound localization. Depending on sound, instrument, and process, performance varies its scope from individual episodes to shared practice.

3.2 Participatory Matrix

By placing Arstein's three levels of participation in the vertical axis of a grid, and our four perspectives of sound making in the horizontal axis, we arrive at the matrix in Table. 3-1.

Table. 3-1: Matrix of Music One Participates In

	Sound	**Instrument**	**Process**	**Performance**
Citizen Power				
Tokenism				
Non-participation				

In the first column, we see different levels of participation with *Sound*. In column 2, we see the levels in *Instrument*. The level of participation represents the choice of sound-making object to produce musical output. While an instrument is highly coupled with the sound it produces, the respective roles of an instrument and sound produced in a musical activity are distinct from a participatory point of view. Column 3 covers different *Processes* for participation, linking method and behavior to sound-making practice. In the last column, we see varying participatory levels in *Performance*. Following our definition of performance as one that is inherently social, we focus on participants' potential for listening linked to playing that create forms of exchange during sound-based activity.

4. Examples

To illustrate the matrix, we situate existing works on the matrix. These works range from traditional musical ensembles through historical avant-garde compositions to sound-based works in the field of media art.

Table. 4-1: Matrix of music one participates in existing musical practice

	Sound	**Instrument**	**Process**	**Performance**
Citizen Power		Drum Circle Dialtone	33 ⅓	Orchestra (Performer)
Tokenism	Drum Circle Orchestra 33 ⅓		Orchestra (Performer) Drum Circle	Drum Circle 33 ⅓
Non-participation	Dialtone	Orchestra 33 ⅓	Orchestra (Audience) Dialtone	Orchestra (Audience) Dialtone

4.1 Classical Orchestra

The classical orchestra typically performs and interprets music notated in score form. The score, as written by the composer is regarded as the original work and the performance is an act of interpretation, a medium to pass the experience of the work to the listener. An instrumentalist in the orchestra engages at several levels of participation. As the score indicates precise instrumentation, participation at the *Instrument* level can be considered <*Non-participation*> in the sense that the instrumentation or orchestration of a traditional symphonic work is not actively modified by performers. Meanwhile, the performer articulates tonal expression through interpretation of dynamics markings in the score. From the point of view of tonal, timbral, thereby *Sound* participation, we can say that the instrumentalist's participation is situated on the matrix at <*Tokenism-Sound*>, that is to say, that the participant (instrumentalist in this case) "hears and is heard" (their interpretation has a real impact on the resulting music), but do not engage at the level of "changing the status quo" (do not actually alter the structure of the composition). The act of performing from a score, and following a conductor is a process we consider to be *<Tokenism-Process>*. Here the notion of "hear and is heard" point out the interaction between conductor and performer. A successful orchestral performance is contingent not only on the precision of the score or the quality of the conductor, but on inter-performer communication that lies at a level of subtlety between the written note and between the conducted beats. The orchestra member's engagement with this act of listening-as-performance is crucial to the success of a concert, and ultimately gives members of the orchestra a form of *<Citizen Power-Performance>*.

The audience of an orchestral concert experience in a concert in a way markedly different from the performers. Members of the audience are typically assigned pre-assigned seating, and thus fixed spatial and temporal occupation at the venue, resulting in *<Non-participation-Process>*. They are not able to influence the event, and so the act of communicative listening amongst audience members remains at *<Non-participation-Performance>* in the matrix.

4.2 Drum Circle

A drum circle is a group of people playing drums together in a self-organized fashion. Stevens [Stevens, 2003: 13] describes the principles of drum circle as follows: "There is no audience", "There is no rehearsal", "There is no right or wrong", "There is no teacher", "It is inclusive", "Spontaneity thrives", and "It's about more than drumming."

In this practice, the sound and the instrument are tightly coupled as a form of extended "drum." People manage their own drumming within the constraints of (*<Tokenism-Sound>*) the drum of their choice (*<Citizen Power-Instrument>*). There is no score, but the pulse and foundational rhythm are set by a facilitator, *<Tokenism-Process>*. The performance has a duality of self-expression and the unity of group rhythm, open contributions to collective rhythm that is nonetheless implicitly guided by a named or unnamed group leader, resulting in *<Tokenism-Performance>*.

4.3 33 ⅓ [Cage, 1969]

33-⅓ is a work by the American composer John Cage. In the work, people enter a room where a set of turntables and more than 200 vinyl records are arranged on tables around a room surrounded by speakers <*Non-participation-Instrument*>. Despite the lack of explicit instructions <*Citizen Power-Process*>, people are able to play records on the turntables, resulting in <*Tokenism-Sound*>. The selection of which record and music to play is left with each participant, who listened to what music other participants were then playing <*Tokenism-Performance*> [Hitchcock, 1992].

4.4 Dialtones (A Telesymphony) [Levin, 2001]

Dialtones (A Telesymphony) is a work whose sounds are produced through the audience's own mobile phones <*Citizen Power-Instrument*>. Participants are assigned the seat at the site and new "ringing tones" <*Non-participation-Sound*> are automatically downloaded to their mobile phones. During the performance, the artists dial the telephone numbers of the audience, causing their mobile phones to ring. While audience member's telephones are used as instruments, they actually have no control in how they are used, resulting in <*Non-participation-Process*>. With their spatial position and sounds from their own phones, people listen spatially distributed melodies and chords determined entirely by their fixed seating and dialing activity by the artists, creating ultimately <*Non-participation-Performance*>.

5. Own Practice

While we are able to apply the matrix to existing musical works, they were most likely not conceived with the forms of participation we describe here in mind. In this section, we present several works from our own artistic practice that were designed specifically to be participatory in the sense proposed here. We begin by describing two projects of The SINE WAVE ORCHESTRA, "Stairway" and "stay", the Chiptune Marching Band (CTMB) and the locative media work Net_Derive. We then compare and contrast the two of The SINE WAVE ORCHESTRA works in detail.

5.1 The Stairway of The SINE WAVE ORCHESTRA

The SINE WAVE ORCHESTRA (SWO) is a sound performance project that creates participatory sound representations since 2002 [http://swo.jp/]. Ken Furudate, Kazuhiro Jo (co-author here), Daisuke Ishida, and Mizuki Noguchi are the core organizers of the project. Under the basic concept that each participant plays a sine wave *<Non-participation-Sound>*, people are invited to create a sea of sine waves as a collective sound representation [Jo et al, 2008].

Table. 5-1: Matrix of music one participates in own practice

	Sound	**Instrument**	**Process**	**Performance**
Citizen Power	Net_Derive	Stairway (own) CTMB	Stairway (provided) CTMB	Stairway CTMB
Tokenism	CTMB		Stairway (own) stay Net_Derive	stay Net_Derive
Non-participation	Stairway stay	Stairway (provided) stay Net_Derive		

In "Stairway", the public are invited to participate via website and mailing list announcements. The organizers provide the participants with 50 instruments to play sine waves *<Non-participation-Instrument>*. The frequency and volume of a sine wave change depending on the amount of light the instrument receives. Some people bring their own instruments (e.g., laptop PCs and synthesizers with speakers) *<Citizen Power-Instrument>* to play sine waves freely at varying frequencies and volumes *<Citizen Power-Process>*.

In a 2004 performance in Tokyo, 200 participants came and played sine waves on the instruments for about two hours at dusk in the large public area of a building atrium. Because of a decrease in sunlight at the end of the day, and the light sensitivity of the instruments provided , people gradually gathered around building lighting fixtures [Figure. 5-1] <*Tokenism-Process*>. Participants moved around the atrium on their own accord and listened to variations of sine waves at each specific location they occupied <*Citizen Power-Performance*>.

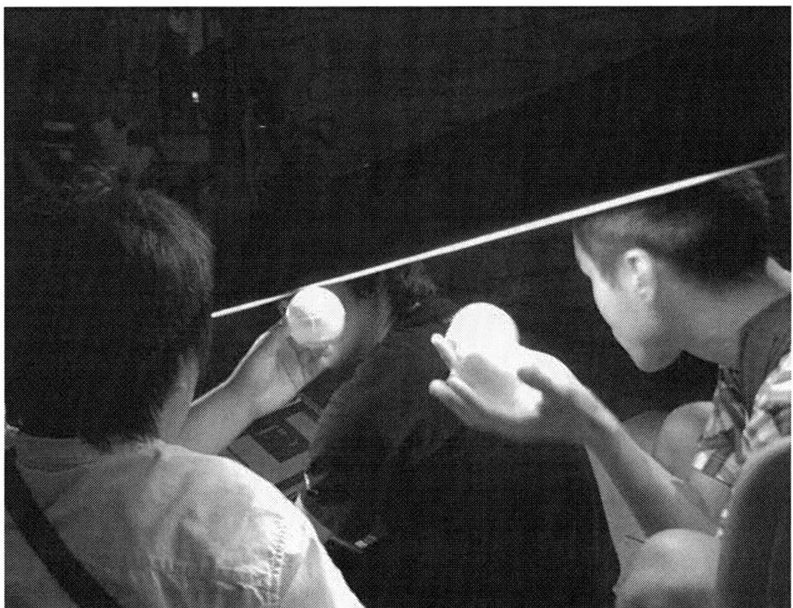

Figure. 5-1: The Stairway of The SINE WAVE ORCHESTRA

5.2 The SINE WAVE ORCHESTRA stay

"stay" consists of a set of controllers and multiple loudspeakers horizontally mounted on the wall in an echoless chamber <*Non-participation-Instrument*> (Figure. 5-2) [Jo et al, 2005]. People select the frequency and the loudspeaker position of a sine wave with knob controllers and then add their sine wave to an accumulated sum, creating a collective sound representation <*Tokenism-Process*>. During a 2005 exhibition, about 8,000 people participated in the work. Depending on the moment of their participation, people hear changes in the collective sound representation from one where each sine wave is discriminable to one where clusters consisting of mutually interfering sine waves to white noise that contains all frequencies <*Tokenism-Performance*>.

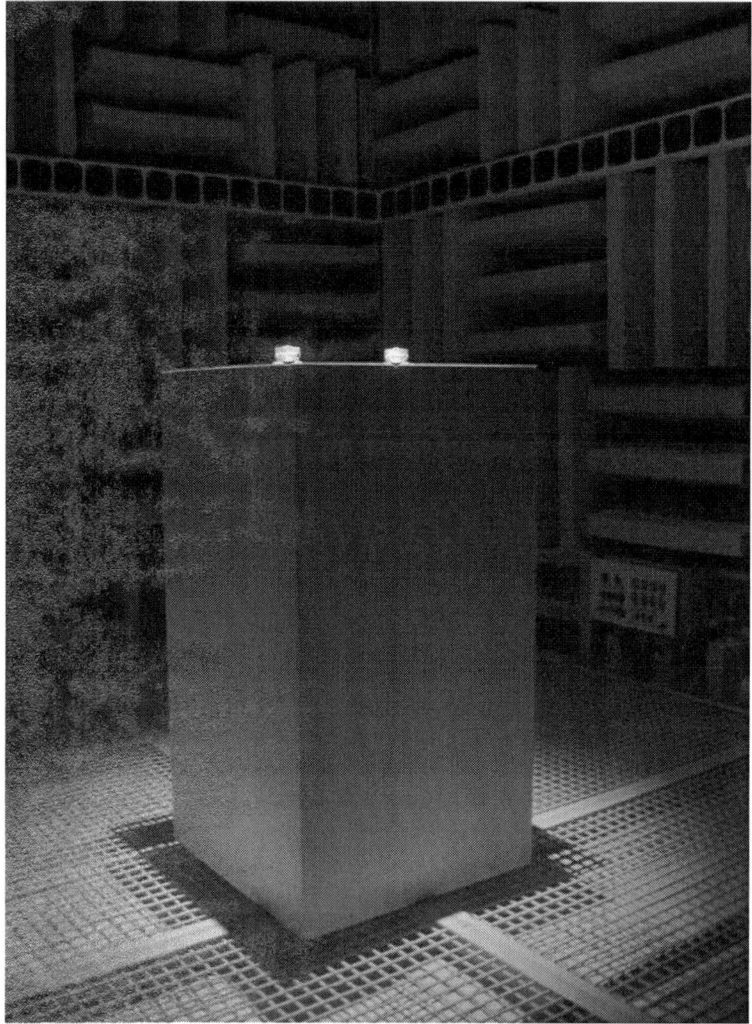

Figure. 5-2: The SINE WAVE ORCHESTRA stay

5.3 Chiptune Marching Band

> Chiptune Marching Band (http://chiptunemarchingband.com) is a public workshop and performance that invites people to learn about self-generated power resources, sound producing electronic circuits, and takes part in collective street performance [Allen, Jo, and Galani, 2009].

The workshop is comprised of a presentation of basic circuit building and instrument fabrication. In building a sound producing electrical ciruit as their own instrument, the participants have a choice of three sensors (i.e. fader, potential meter, and photo resistor) to incorporate into their instrument, as well as a choice of capacitor value that determines the tonal range of the instrument. This choice of component is integrated into a basic fixed circuit, so represents *<Tokenism-Sound>*. Participants fit their circuit with the cardboard tube and fabricate and personalize their instrument with paint, markers, and stickers in their own way, resulting in *<Citizen Power-Instrument>*.

After the participants finish the workshop, they enter into discussion about how to organize a street performance with their instruments *<Citizen Power-Process>*. Following the discussion, participants form a "marching band" and parade in the streets as a public performance *<Citizen Power-Performance>*.

5.4 Net_Derive

Net_Derive is a multiuser mobile music work in the tradition of locative media art [Tanaka and Gemeinboeck, 2008]. Participants are provided with a white scarf containing two mobile phones and a GPS module, an instrument inspired by wearable computing technologies *<Non-participation-Instrument>*.

Participants explore the neighborhood surrounding the exhibition gallery. The GPS coordinates of the participants are used to generate a series of polyrhythmic pulses, where the speed depends on relative proximity of up to three participants. Certain latitude/longitude combinations also trigger nonsense voice commands, instructing the participant to stop, turn, or continue. As the participant chooses to heed or ignore these instructions *<Tokenism-Process>*, a trace of his path is carved out in the city.

There is also an audio upstream from each mobile serving as a roaming live microphone with each participant *<Citizen Power-Sound>*. The street sounds feeds a server-side music engine, is cut up, looped, processed, and mixed algorithmically, and layered under the blips and voice commands. This applies notions of musique concrète to machine processes, composing automatically with real world sounds. With the mobile participant receiving this "concretized" mix streamed back in real time, the process of becomes real time, live, and in direct connection to the participant's immediate surroundings <*Tokenism-Performance*>.

6. Contrast of two works of The SINE WAVE ORCHESTRA

In 1822, the French mathematician, Fourier, discovered that sine waves could be used as the basic components to form nearly any periodic signal [Fourier, 1955]. Based on his theory, SWO regards each sine wave as individual persons and the collective sound representation as community. The interference and resonance of sine waves depict the relationship of the participants much as that of individual sine wave components in a complex timbral amalgam. Although all SWO works use the same *Sound* (i.e. sine waves) as a starting point, the two works described here employ different *Instruments* and *Processes*. The differences result in different forms of listening and playing activity as *Performance*.

In "Stairway", as the provided instrument can not produce sound with the small amount of light at sunset, we observed that participants gathered around lamps and other light sources with their instruments. As the amount of light that defines the frequency heard, local variations in luminosity produced small frequency differences resulting in beating patterns from mutual interfering sine waves. We also observed that some participants dynamically changed the volume by illuminating the instrument with a flashlight. We also saw that some of the participants shared their knowledge and showed others how to play, negotiating ways of playing the instruments, whether they be those provided by the artists or brought by the participants. Some passersbys stopped to ask the participants what they were doing and finished by taking part in the work.

In "stay", we provide an instrument for a large number of exhibition visitors. Each participant listens to the sound that other participants had played, and one by one, produces a sine wave at different moments in time. Every time a participant uses the instrument, one sine wave is added to the collective sound. The work uses 116 speakers as a part of the instrument. Each speaker outputs a cluster that consists of mutual interfering sine waves with different frequencies from different participants. Therefore, depending on where the participant stands in the room relative to the location of the multiple speakers, what is heard changes dynamically.

In each work of SWO, the collective sound representation actively changes its state through user involvement. The sound and instrument act as dynamic interactive systems to include output from the participants [Cornock and Edmonds, 1973]. In a traditional classical orchestra, skilled performers produce collective sound representations by playing instruments on which they have practiced for long periods of time. In SWO works, the instrument is an unfamiliar device to the participants. By restricting its sonic possibilities, participants quickly learn to play it in the course of their participation.

7. Discussion

We have mapped out a matrix of musical participation that correlates social levels of empowerment with different aspects of sound creation. We explored how the matrix could help to understand the nature of the styles and the dynamics of musical participation. We have discussed different facets of sound making practice through three levels of participation.

The matrix enables us to understand the transfer of authority in existing sound making practices. Eco, in describing open works, notes a shift of initiative from the composer to the individual performer [Eco, 1959]. He mentions the difference between works that the composer arranges in a closed, well-defined manner before presenting it to the listener, and works that are brought to their conclusion by the performer with multiple formal possibilities of the distribution of their elements.

The aim of this paper was to look beyond the fixed roles of participants (i.e. composer, performer, audience). We are interested in works with indefinite boundaries between roles and dynamics of participation where people subjectively engage with sound representation through listening and simultaneously engage with the creation of sound. Each person is a listener of others, and a performer to others. In these works, the evolution of the collective sound representation is unpredictable and depends on the total involvement of the participants [Ascott, 1966].

The traditional role of the artist, composer, or writer is thus called into question; it may no longer necessary to assume that he/she is a specialist in art - rather he is a catalyst of creative activity [Cornock and Edmonds, 1973]. She intervenes in each perspective of sound making practice by sculpting levels of participation. The resulting representation is produced by the participants as much as it is by the artist who has conceived the system. Our work is consistent with ideas of shared knowledge where "every posting is just another person's version of the truth; every fiction is just another person's version of the facts [Keen, 2007]." In the paper, we offer the matrix for the *Music One Participates In* as a basis of further discussion to cultivate emergence in creative practice.

Acknowledgements

We would like to thank Jamie Allen, Areti Galani, the students on the Digital Media program at Newcastle University, and Culture Lab staff for their participation in and support of this research. We would also like to thank the other members of the projects and all participants in our work.

References

Allen, J., Jo, K., and Galani, A. (2009) An Ecology of Practice: Chiptune Marching Band, Proceeding of ACM Creativity and Cognition Conference 2009, ACM Press (to be published).

ASA, (1960) Acoustical terminology, s.1.1, American standards association.

Ascott, R. (1966) Behaviorist art and cybernetic vision, Cybernetica 9, 4, pp.247–264.

Auslander, P (2000) Fluxus Art-Amusement: The Music of the Future? [revised and expanded version], Contours of the Theatrical Avant-Garde: Performance and Textuality, ed. James Harding. Ann Arbor: University of Michigan Press.

Arnstein, S. R. (1969) A Ladder of Citizen Participation, Journal of the American Institute of Planners, Vol. 35, No. 4, pp.216-224.

Attali, J. (1985) Noise: The Political Economy of Music, trans. Brian Massumi, University of Minnesota Press.

Bailey, D. (1992) Improvisation: Its Nature and Practice in Music, New York: Da Capo Press.

Barthes, R. (1977) Musica pratica, In Image-Music-Text, Hill and Wang, New York, pp.149-154.

Bishop, C. (2006) Introduction//Viewers as Producers, Bishop, C. ed., Participation, Documents of Contemporary Art, MIT Press, pp.10-17.

Blaine, T. and Fels, S. (2003) Collaborative Musical Experiences for Novices, Journal of New Music Research, 32:4, pp.411-428.

Bongers, B. (2007) Electronic musical Instruments: Experiences of a new Luthier, Leonardo Music Journal 17, MIT Press, pp.9-16.

Cage, J. (1969), 33 ⅓, November 21, 1969 at the campus of the University of California at Davis. http://www.johncage.info/workscage/331_3.html

Cornock, S. and Edmonds, E. (1973) The creative process where the artist is amplified or superseded by the computer, Leonardo 6, 1, MIT Press, pp.11–16.

Eco, U. (1959) The Poetics of the Open Work, Cox, C. ed., Audio Culture: Audio Culture: Readings in Modern Music (1999), New York: The Continuum International Publishing Group, pp.167-175.

Fourier, J. (1955) The Analytical Theory of Heat, New York, Dover Publications, Inc. (Original work: Theorie Analytique de la Chaleur, Paris, 1822.)

Goffman, E. (1959) The Presentation of Self in Everyday Life, New York:Doubleday.

Hitchcock, H. W. (1992) I.S.A.M. Matters, Institute for Studies in American Music Newsletter, Volume XXXVII, No. 2, Spring 2008, pp.6-7.

Hunt, A., Wanderley, M. M., and Paradis, M. (2002) The importance of parameter mapping in electronic instrument design, In Proceedings of the Conference on New Interfaces for Musical Expression (NIME-02), pp.149-154.

Jo, K., Furudate, K., Ishida, D., and Noguchi, M. (2008) Transition of instruments in The SINE WAVE ORCHESTRA, ACM Computers in Entertainment, ACM Press, Vol.6, 4, pp.1-18.

Jo, K., Furudate, K., Ishida, D., and Noguchi, M. (2005) The SINE WAVE ORCHESTRA stay, Proceedings of ACM Multimedia 2005, ACM Press, pp.571-573.

Keen, A. (2007) The Cult of the Amateur: How Today's Internet is Killing Our Culture, London: Nicholas Brealey Publishing.

Lave, J. and Wenger, E. (1991) Situated Learning: Legitimate Peripheral Participation, Cambridge University Press, Cambridge, UK.

Levin, G. (2001) Dialtones (A Telesymphony), Catalogue of Ars Electronica, Linz, Austria.

McClary, S. (1985) The Politics of Silence and Sound, in Attali, Noise, p.158.

Schechner, R. (1988) Performance Theory, Routledge New York.

Small, C. (1998) Musicking: The meanings of performing and listening, Hanover: University Press of New England.

Stevens, C. (2003) The Art and Heart of Drum Circles. Milwaukee, Wis: Hal Leonard Corporation.

Tanaka, A. and Gemeinboeck, P. (2008) Net_Dérive: Conceiving and Producing a Locative Media Artwork In Goggin, G. and Hjorth, L. (eds.) Mobile Technologies: Communication into Media. London: Routledge, pp.174-186.

Tanaka, A. (2009) Sensor-Based Musical Instruments and Interactive Music, The Oxford handbook of computer music, Oxford University Press, pp.233-257.

Weinberg, G. (2005) Interconnected Musical Networks, Towards a Theoretical Framework, Computer Music Journal, MIT Press, Vol. 29:2, pp.23-39.

CHAPTER FOUR

THE VITRUVIAN WORLD: A CASE STUDY IN CREATIVE HYBRIDISATION OF VIRTUAL, PHYSICAL AND NETWORKED SPACE

MICHAEL TAKEO MAGRUDER

In February 2007, Turbulence,[1] a leading international portal and commissioner of networked art, released a call for proposals seeking to "challenge our preconceptions of what constitutes *reality*" within this age of interconnected and shared environments:

> Information and telecommunications technologies allow us to be continuously connected via the Internet or mobile networks. We engage one another via e-mail, chat, the interlinked pages of the World Wide Web and SMS. We create identities, and forge relationships and communities. Boundaries between real space and virtual space blur; near and far reverse themselves. Passive consumption of art is replaced by the *performative*–art that requires *(inter)action*, and involves time and space. (*Mixed Realities* call for proposals, March 2007)

The result of this call was an international exhibition and symposium, entitled *Mixed Realities,*[2] curated by Jo-Anne Green, Co-Director of Turbulence. Five creative teams[3] were commissioned to produce artworks that would engage users across three distinct environments: the online virtual world of *Second Life*, a traditional gallery space and the Internet, via the Turbulence website. Although art events of this nature would soon become relatively commonplace within New Media Art practice, *Mixed Realities* was one of the earliest exhibitions–if not the first–actively to address the purposeful blending of these three types of spaces.

Fig. 1 Five proposals selected for *Mixed Realities*: (from left to right) *Caterwall*, *Imaging Beijing*, *No Matter*, *Remote* and *The Vitruvian World.*

Towards an artistically-viable 3D shared virtual environment

As a concept, *Mixed Realities* was not revolutionary, but rather, an evolutionary extension of earlier, artistic trends of the previous two decades. The appropriation of emerging technologies from the telecommunication and computer industries was, and still remains, a defining characteristic of New Media Art and Performance. During this period, artists working in the fields of Internet and Telematic Art had utilised network infrastructures such as the World Wide Web and ISDN video conferencing systems for the conceptualisation, production and dissemination of artistic works and interventions. Considerable bodies of three-dimensional (3D) art were created on both the Web[4] via *ActiveX* browser plugins such as *Cortona VRML* and *Adobe Shockwave* and game platforms such as the *Unreal Engine* (Epic Games, 1998-).

Due to the technological limitations of such systems, these virtual or mixed-reality spaces were, for the most part, discrete systems with rigid and often immovable boundaries defined by the inherent characteristics of the media. The restricted nature of these artworks often created clear divisions between the spectator/user experience and the wider environment in which they were situated. Net Art could not escape from the frame of the web browser and telematic embraces could not materialise without complex audio-visual studio facilities. As isolated events contained within, but intrinsically detached from everyday life, such artworks pointed to the need for new, more sophisticated technologies that would afford a greater-degree of cultural integration and mainstream exposure.

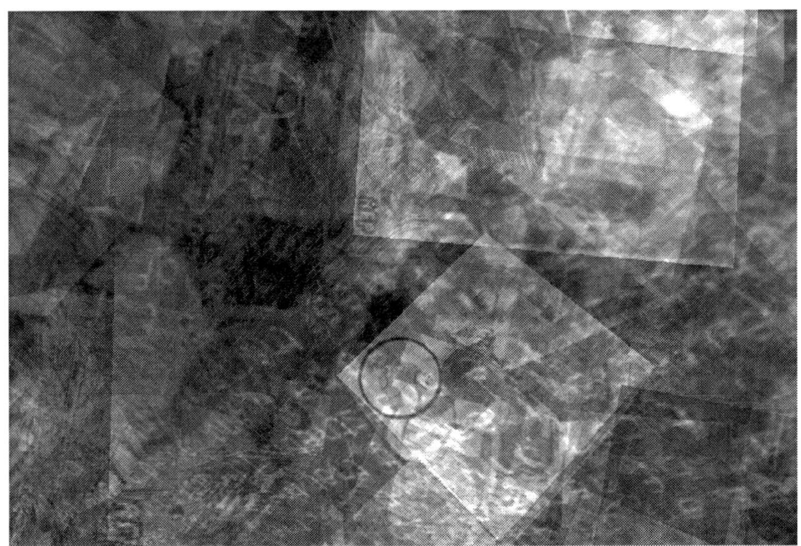

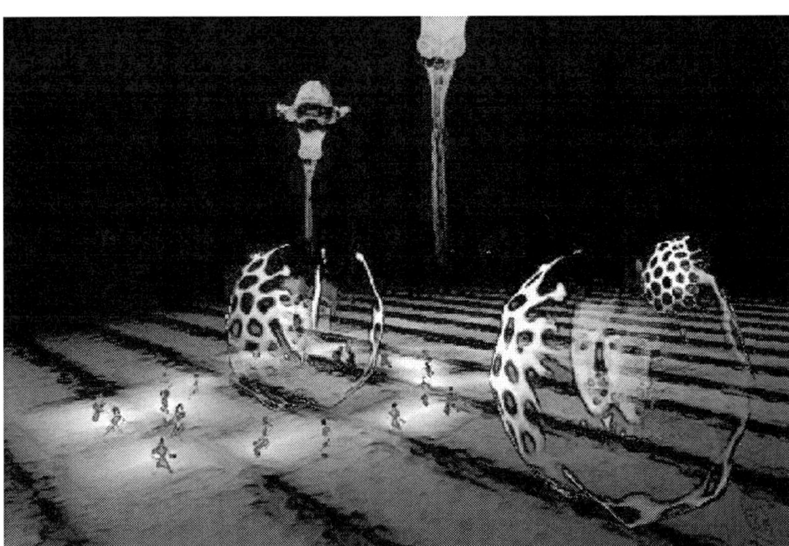

Real-time 3D art: Fig. 2 (above) *Data_cosm* by M. Takeo Magruder, 2005, *VRML/Flash/Java* and Fig. 3 (below) *Home Dictate* by Ivor Diosi, 2003, *Unreal Engine*.

As the early digital telephony services such as Dial-up and ISDN were supplanted by affordable broadband connections such as xDSL, applications began to emerge that took advantage of these exponentially-higher data transmission rates. With these enhancements to the global network infrastructure, the web began shifting from a pull-based information repository into an application-rich Web 2.0 platform through which users could shape to a much greater degree their own online experiences. This conjunction of inexpensive broadband with a rapidly-increasing pool of web-based applications engendered the rise of a new, mainstream online-sharing culture. Multi-user platforms such as *MySpace*, *Facebook*, *YouTube*, *Flickr*, *Twitter* and *Wikipedia* were inevitable by-products of a media-rich, interconnected net-space that both influenced and reflected the needs and desires of Information Age society. The isolated individual experience was increasingly replaced by social encounters in shared virtual environments, and many of the processes of content creation and publishing that were once solely in the domain of media corporations became accessible to individuals and communities willing to create within self-authored or inter-authored[5] frameworks.

The impact of the Web 2.0 paradigm on 3D graphics

Advances in consumer-level graphics facilitated the rise of 3D platforms within home computing during the 1990s. For the skilled, the creation of single-user virtual realms and objects for the Web was possible through formats like Virtual Reality Modeling Language (VRML). Although the subsequent generation of multi-user environments such as *Active Worlds* (1995), *The Mirror* (1997) and *Adobe Atmosphere* (1999) extended the potential of online virtual worlds by incorporating facilities for customisable realms, group chat and user-generated content, uptake of these platforms was limited to small communities interested in 3D web technologies. It was not until the entertainment industry's Massively Multiplayer Online Role-Playing Game (MMORPG) genre adopted 3D graphics that general public awareness of 3D Shared Virtual Environments (SVEs) became more commonplace (Magruder, 2008). In contrast to the low-usage of previous academic and commercial ventures, games such as *EverQuest* (Sony Online Entertainment, 1999) attracted nearly five hundred thousand players to a persistent virtual realm. The game industry's domination of the format continued into the new millennium with releases like *Final Fantasy XI* (Square Enix, 2002), *RuneScape* (Jagex Ltd., 2003), *Lineage II* (NCsoft, 2003) and *World of Warcraft* (Blizzard Entertainment, 2004) that enticed millions of individuals to venture

3D SVEs: Fig. 4 (above) fantasy adventures in *EverQuest*, 1999 and Fig. 5 (below) Le Mont Saint-Michel island by Moeka Kohime in *Second Life*, 2009.

into 3D SVEs for the first time. Non-game use of the format continued, but would remain in obscurity until Linden Lab's public launch of *Second Life* in 2003.

Second Life's c.1.7 million active users in 2009, though not in the league of chart-topping MMORPGs such as *World of Warcraft* (c.11.5m) or *RuneScape* (c.8.5m), is by any reasonable measure still a very notable success, particularly as, unlike most MMORPGs, it does not provide an overarching game narrative. Rather, it is a persistent virtual world occupied by avatars (personalised graphical representations of individual users in the virtual environment) and consists, for the most part of buildings, objects and effects created by its "residents".

The extensive media coverage of *Second Life* and its commercial success, particularly its significant uptake by non-gaming communities, was the result of a convergence of several key factors. Linden Lab aligned *Second Life* with the Web 2.0 'do-it-yourself' culture by associating the platform with the trademark phrase: "your world, your imagination" and unlike the prevailing subscription-based models of competing systems, entry into the virtual world and full customisation of avatars was completely free for all end users. As with the immensely successful MMORPGs, *Second Life* placed the virtual self at the forefront of the virtual experience. The platform allowed individuals to construct highly-personalised and detailed avatars and encouraged residents to work, play and express themselves in ways that were either impractical or impossible in their 'real' lives.

From a technical perspective, Linden Lab deviated from previous attempts at hosting 3D SVEs on distributed independent servers and adopted a unified grid architecture similar to those deployed within the games industry. This centralised approach provided residents with a consistent quality of service and ensured that all locations within *Second Life* were continuously online. Linden Lab also developed an extensive in-world set of building and scripting tools that could easily be used by *Second Life* neophytes, while simultaneously offering those individuals with advanced 3D authoring skills the means to fabricate complex items and environments.

These conditions attracted a diverse range of interest groups to the emerging metaverse.[6] Established companies rushed to develop brand presence within *Second Life*, while entrepreneurs developed new business models, resulting in vast virtual shopping centres and innovative leisure areas in hopes of tempting residents to indulge in the latest virtual luxuries and services. Educators and artists from numerous disciplines, exploiting the environment's native support for undertaking distributed content creation and performance, began to utilise the platform for new modes of collaborative practice and experimental research. *Second Life's* incorporation of these types of 'real-world' activities into its core experience engendered a sense amongst its users that the platform could both facilitate and advance 'first-life' projects and ambitions. These factors distinguished *Second Life* from other publically-available platforms of the time and helped to precipitate a critical mass of registered users that evolved into a sustainable community.

Referencing antiquity to reflect upon the contemporary

The emergence of *Second Life* as a viable platform for creative production and research provided artists working within New Media discourses opportunities to address concepts such as those proposed by Turbulence's *Mixed Realities* initiative. *Second Life's* accessibility and the user-centric nature of the environment opened new avenues to update and extend practice within the field of networked Virtual Art. Practitioners viewed the arrival of *Second Life* as a means to overcome the technological inhibitors of previous generations of Web and games platforms; their work would no longer necessarily consist of isolated virtual microcosms with limited or non-existent interaction between users.

The Vitruvian World (Magruder/Baker/Steele, 2007),[7] one of the five projects selected for *Mixed Realities*, created a multi-nodal installation that simultaneously occurred across virtual, physical and network spaces, and also linked the three discrete environments into an overarching single 'reality' in which the overall experience was dependent, in part, on the interaction between users of the different realms. *The Vitruvian World* was not only conceptually positioned within contemporary New Media Art discourse concerning networks and the formation of mixed/augmented realities, but was also situated within the tradition of art appropriating new visual technologies and methodologies in order to expand the expressive potential of the creative process.

The notions of illusion and immersion, the fundamental basis of all 3D virtual realities and environments, are artistic concepts with lineages that can be traced back through Western art history to the panoramic Roman wall-paintings from antiquity (Grau, 2003), and arguably, even to the pre-historic cave paintings from Palaeolithic sites like Lascaux (Rheingold,

Ancient immersive and illusionistic spaces: Fig. 6 (above) Roman frescos, Triclinium 14, Villa of Oplontis and Fig. 7 (below) Palaeolithic cave paintings, Lascaux.

1991). In these settings, our ancestors projected their consciousness into spaces existing beyond the physical walls of their luxurious villas and cave dwellings–the scenographic designs and vistas acting as agents of imagination for earlier ages. Considering that these communal environments were designed to promote and enhance social interaction and shared experience, perhaps past architectural theories governing their construction could still inform the creation and usage of their contemporary equivalents, even the most cutting-edge virtual platforms.

In the 1st century BC, Vitruvius, a Roman writer, architect and engineer, authored his treatise *De Architectura* (also known as *The Ten Books of Architecture*), which after rediscovery in 1414 by Bracciolini, became a major influence on the architecture and art of the Renaissance, Baroque, Neoclassical and beyond. Within its pages, Vitruvius outlined specific formulae for building structures based on the guiding principles of *firmitas*, *utilitas*, *venustas*–strength, utility and beauty. Vitruvius theorised that architecture was intrinsically linked to nature and existed as a constructed imitation of cosmic order. The most well-known interpretation of this postulate, the *Vitruvian Man* by da Vinci, depicts the human form in unity with the square and circle–representing material and spiritual existence respectively. Given the relevance of this tripartite union to issues surrounding virtual bodies, mixed-realities and distributed presences within contemporary networked culture, it was conceivable that Vitruvius' theories on proportion and architecture could inform artistic investigations within 3D SVEs like *Second Life*.

Examination of this hypothesis required close consultation with academic scholars well-versed in the interpretation of Vitruvius' writings and the application of his theories within visualisation-based procedural modelling. In 2005, Drew Baker, Senior Research Fellow at King's College London and long-standing member of the institution's visualisation lab,[8] had extracted from *De Architectura*[9] all passages relating to the proportions of Roman temple construction and translated this information into a series of recursive equations that could be codified within a software environment. The resulting VRML model, *Vitruvian Ideal Temples* (Baker, 2006), allowed users to initiate transformation of a virtual temple through real-time modification of its structural variables and architectural measurements.

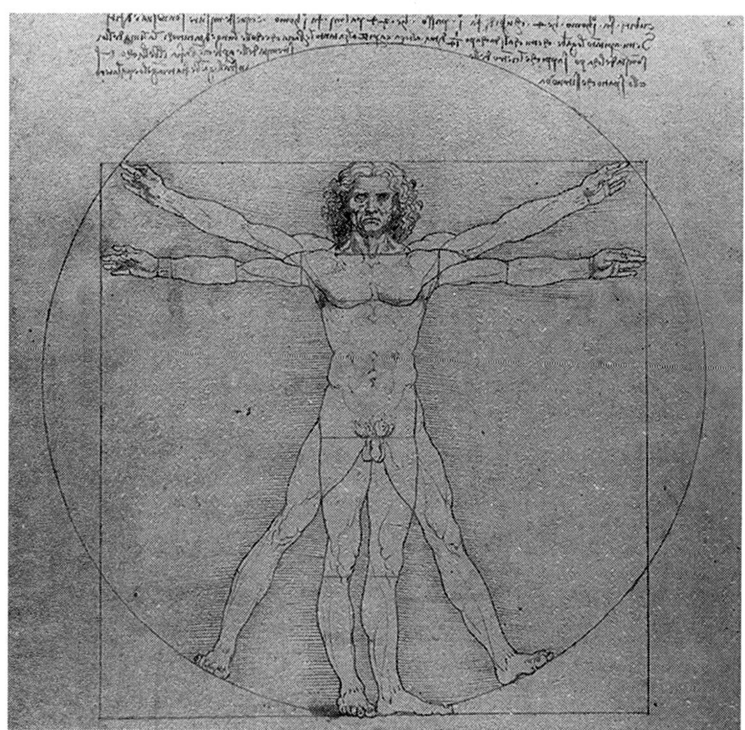

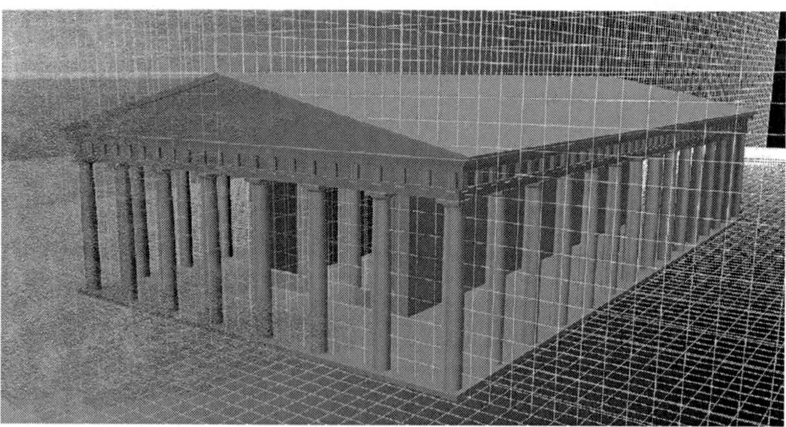

Visual interpretations of Vitruvius' theories: Fig. 8 (above) *Vitruvian Man* by Leonardo da Vinci, c.1487 and Fig. 9 (below) *Vitruvian Ideal Temples*, D. Baker, 2006.

Equally important to this humanities expertise was in-depth knowledge of the technical infrastructure required for establishing interconnectivity between the proposed virtual, physical and network spaces. Data input/output problems associated with *Second Life's* proprietary closed architecture were well-documented, and in most instances, could only be resolved through custom hacks[10] and the addition of other software layers to the platform. David Steele, a leading independent programmer and systems architect for the US telecommunications industry, had worked in software development since the mid 1990s, during which time he pioneered the pairing of cutting-edge client systems to existing corporate infrastructures. Steele's expertise in data mining, processing, transmission and integration could address the project's technical challenges and facilitate the creation of an innovative schema for interlinking the three environments.

An installation of three spaces and three bodies

The Vitruvian World aggregated contemporary art practice, humanities research and software engineering into an interdisciplinary project influenced conceptually by the team's previous artistic work using online 3D platforms[11] and methodologically by academically-orientated initiatives such as *Theatron 3.*[12] The project embodied a creative intersection between Magruder's New Media Art practice, Baker's research and Steele's technological development, resulting in an aesthetic environment accurately composed according to Vitruvian proportions and technically constructed with recursive, networked interplay between its elements.

For the three environments in which *The Vitruvian World* was to coexist, the team envisaged three distinct bodies, each intrinsically linked to one of the realms. The virtual world of *Second Life* would be host to the **Avatar**, the physical space of the gallery would be conjoined with a **Puppet** (a virtual entity constructed by the team for use by members of the visiting public) and the connecting network would be interlinked by a **Doll** (a virtual shell devoid of all presence and integrated into the core fabric of the installation). In addition, these bodies would be defined by their capacity to express will within a system (agency) and to convey the decisions of their creators and/or users within the mixed-reality environment.

Fig. 10 *The Vitruvian World*: blending virtual, physical and network environments.

The virtual (realm of the Avatar)

In *Second Life*, there is no material difference between environments, architectures and bodies as these elements are constructed from the same components. Virtual wind, light, buildings, plants and avatars are all created from a common pool of prims,[13] scripts and media streams, many of which are user-generated, while others are native artefacts of the platform itself. The virtual realm is not bound by the laws of the physical universe, but rather, is shaped into a "living space"[14] according to the intentions of its system architects, world builders and residents.

This fluid metaverse is the domain of its avatar inhabitants–the projected extensions of a disparate collection of individuals channelling their consciousnesses into the shared environment. For these beings, the project created a Utopian world of idealised forms drawing on Vitruvius' strict instructions for temple construction. Occupying an entire sim[15] within *Second Life*, the space consists of a set of architectural structures forming a central square enclosed by lush grounds and a forest of trees arranged in a pair of concentric rings. The environment's aesthetics are informed by hyper-real textures reminiscent of polished stone and vegetation, while the

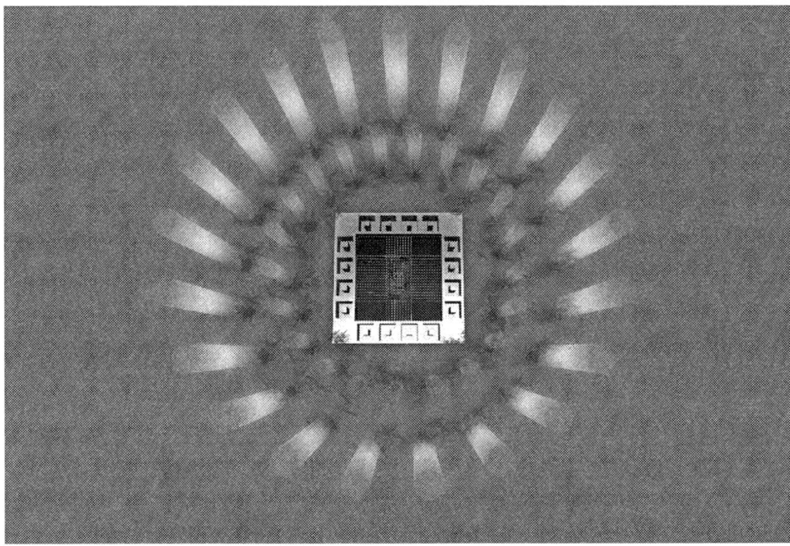

The virtual: Fig. 11 (above) aerial view of *The Vitruvian World* and Fig. 12 (below) night time view of an Avatar exploring *The Vitruvian World*.

synthetic sound of wind and columns of white light emanate from the surrounding forest enhancing the ambience of the virtual land.

The morphology of the world is based upon the unchanging diameter of a single replicated column structure, and every component of the realm is proportionally and compositionally related to this fixed seed. Many of the world's objects are embedded with programmatic functionality that senses the presence of individual avatars. The interactions between these components and the virtual bodies trigger oscillations within the space as determined by the underlying Vitruvian framework. Human decision, through the agency of the avatar, counterbalances the deterministic foundations of the world, and creates a structured, but unpredictable aesthetic flux.

The physical (realm of the Puppet)

Within this virtual world there is a small enclosure where avatars may not venture, and although the environment appears undivided, it is apportioned into two symbiotic parts. The surrounding world for the avatars encircles an isolated space–a finite microcosm enveloped by the endless metaverse. This domain is home to a solitary human form covered with the same textures as the structures of its neighbouring architectural environment and devoid of any bodily traces of personalisation. Intrinsically linked to its prison-like realm, this being often appears suspended and lifeless, as if it exists without a person's soul. It is a puppet, a generic vessel for human agency, waiting to be animated.

Spanning countless nodes across vast data networks, the confined virtual space is linked to a remote physical location in which visitors are confronted by the puppet's senses. Through a dual high-definition corner projection array and a 5.1 audio system, individuals become immersed in its visual and aural surroundings. Passive spectators can become active participants by using a *Wiimote*[16] that rests upon a small plinth located in front of the projection. This hacked game controller allows a person to assume control of the puppet and instil their will into its lifeless shell.

The intentions of the creative team and random users intertwine as the puppet's actions are sensed by the environment, and as with the avatars above, initiate transformations within the virtual space. A dialogue of human choices mixing with algorithmic processes ensues, with each half of the realm exerting different influences upon the world as a whole.

The physical: Fig. 13 (above) portrait of the Puppet and Fig. 14 (below) view from the eyes of the Puppet.

The network (realm of the Doll)

The barrier separating the two distinct realms within the world is more than just a divider of space, as traces of the world's history linger on its surface as time unfolds within the virtual expanse. It is a living boundary reflecting the past dialogue between the visiting avatars and the puppet's masters. These memories are not aggregated by the barrier itself as it is only a receptacle for information flow. The agent of this process is a third entity that resides within a hidden place. Resting atop a simple cube as if in contemplation, its body, stripped of all human essence and free from any influence, contains no consciousness. It is a doll within the world, an object within the metaverse serving as a collector of memories and recorder of histories.

Everything that ventures within the doll's dislocated view is captured and remembered. The images it records are transmitted out across the network to a server that algorithmically processes them into a serialised data stream. This material is then redistributed back into the network where it is accessed by the *Second Life* grid and reabsorbed into its source environment. Fragments of mediated time are overlaid upon the ever-changing boundary as the doll continues to record the world, thus forming a reflexive loop in which the real-time documentation process and resulting archive become part of that which is being recorded.

Visitors to the virtual realm are not the only ones able to view the machinic stream of consciousness. These recollections, like the network that transmits them, are part of the public domain and can be accessed by any web browser connected to the Internet. Individuals visiting the Turbulence website can view a webpage containing an embedded Flash applet that intercepts the data stream and transmutes it into a flowing visual narrative. The applet acquires random images processed during the previous hour and algorithmically remixes them into a non-linear sequence. Moments of the current time are blended with the recent past to generate a forever-shifting composition reminiscent of a painterly montage.

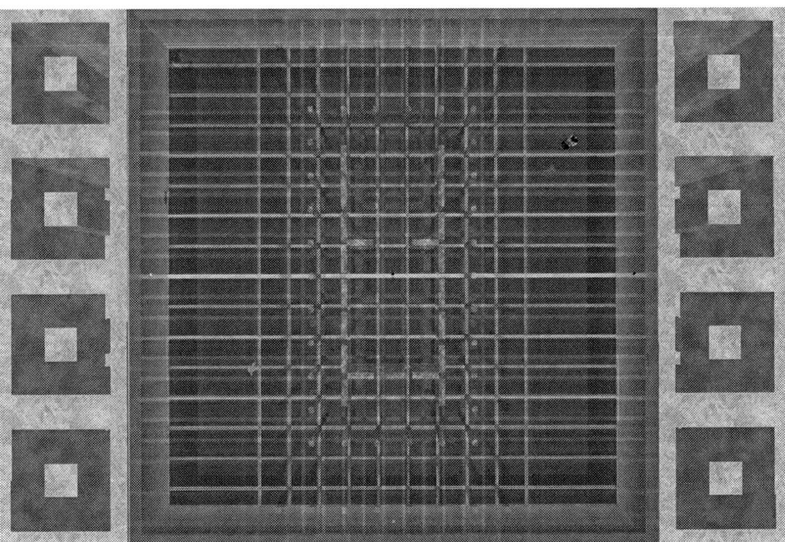

The network: Fig. 15 (above) portrait of the Doll and Fig. 16 (below) view from the eyes of the Doll.

Towards an artistically-sustainable 3D shared virtual environment

Installations such as *The Vitruvian World* exemplify the potential of the current generation of 3D SVEs for mixed-reality artworks and hint at the creative possibilities which may arise from future technological advances in the area. However, there are serious issues and challenges facing the users, developers and owners of these systems as the facilities they provide have superseded many accepted working-practices based on older traditions and media. As with popular social networking sites like *MySpace* and *Facebook*, 3D SVEs are currently embroiled in controversies regarding access to and ownership of user-generated content. Through ethically-questionable terms and conditions of service, platform suppliers are coercing their users to relinquish many of the legal rights historically given to authors and creators.

In addition, unlike many Web 2.0 platforms in which the user-generated experience is completely free, the majority of 3D SVEs such as *Second Life* and *Active Worlds* levy substantial charges for the ownership and maintenance of virtual land required for the creation and dissemination of content. This commercial reality, exacerbated by the current global financial crisis, has led to the formation of a new digital divide amongst user communities in which those without sufficient financial resources are severely restricted in their ability to use these systems for their research and practice, and indeed the commercial longevity of platforms like *Second Life* is as yet unknown. The introduction of open source alternatives like *OpenSimulator*[17] has helped address these concerns and alleviate the intellectual property issues and financial restrictions of their commercial counterparts, but as with many new open source technologies, the environment lacks the infrastructure refinements–most notably a persistent shared grid–to be considered as an entirely satisfactory solution for general public use.

Despite their problems and shortcomings, it is important to acknowledge that the current generation of 3D SVEs has opened-up numerous avenues for collaborative and creative engagement in the Arts and Humanities. While artists and performers will continue to anticipate and exploit future technological developments, our minds and imaginations still have yet fully to digest the seemingly infinite possibilities that shared 3D worlds already offer.

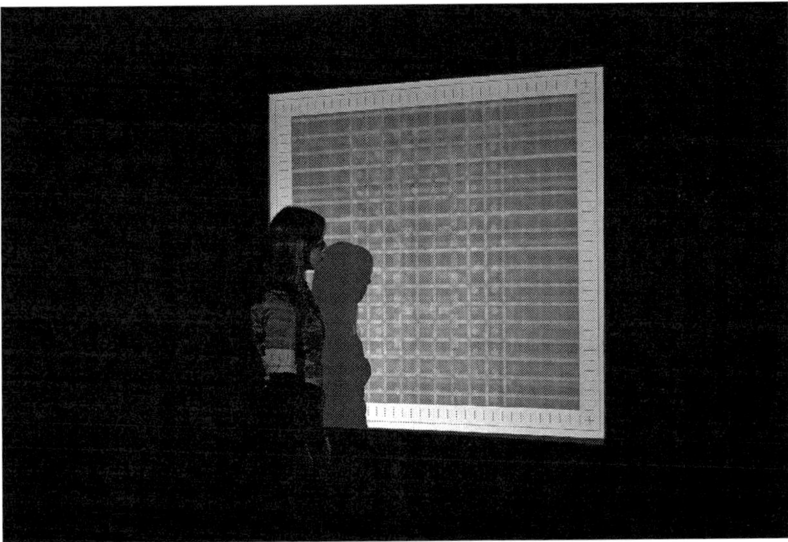

Figs. 17 and 18 *The Vitruvian World* as part of the *Virtual/Physical Bodies* exhibition, Centre des Arts, Enghien-les-Bains, Paris, France, 2008.

References

Appia, Adolphe (1921), *L'Œuvre d'art vivant*, Geneva/Paris.

Baker, Drew (2006), *Vitruvian Ideal Temples* [web-based 3D visualisation], www.datascape.org/dbaker/vit/, accessed on 06/2009.

Beacham, Richard (1993), *Adolphe Appia: Texts on Theatre*, Routledge.

Boddington, Ghislaine (2006), *The Weave*, in Christopher Bannerman, Joshua Sofaer and Jane Watts (eds), *Navigating the Unknown: The Creative Process in Contemporary Performing Arts*, Middlesex University Press, pp. 70-89.

Grau, Oliver (2003), *Virtual Art: From Illusion to Immersion*, The MIT Press.

Magruder, M. Takeo, Baker, D. & Steele, D. (2007), *The Vitruvian World* [artwork], www.turbulence.org/Works/vitruvianworld/, accessed on 06/2009.

Magruder, Michael Takeo (2007), *Isolation to Population, Microcosm to Environment: The Transition from VRML to Second Life as a Platform for Networked 3D Arts Practice*, in Johannes Birringer, Thomas Dumke and Klaus Nikolai (eds), *Die Welt als Virtuelles Environment*, Dresden: TMA Hellerau, pp. 100-114.

—. (2008), *Virtual Me(s): Avatar Embodiment in the Console Age*, in Dominique Roland, Ghislaine Boddington and Emmanuel Cuisinier (eds), *Virtual/Physical Bodies*, Centre des Arts d'Enghien-les-Bains, pp. 34-41.

Morgan, Morris Hicky (1914), *Vitruvius: The Ten Books on Architecture*, Harvard University Press.

Rheingold, Howard (1991), *Virtual Reality*, Summit Books.

Smith, Thomas Gordon (2003), *Vitruvius on Architecture*, Monacelli Press.

Stephenson, Neil (1992), *Snow Crash*, Bantam Books.

Notes

[1] A project of New Radio and Performing Arts, Inc. (NRPA) launched in 1996 to support the creation and dissemination of networked art. (www.turbulence.org)

[2] www.turbulence.org/mixed_realities/

[3] *Caterwall* by P. Proske with assistance from A. Baguinski and B. Lichtenegger, *Imaging Beijing* by J. C. Freeman, *No Matter* by S. Kildall and V. Scott, *Remote* by N. Donaldson, U. Haque, A. Hasegawa and G. Tremmel, *The Vitruvian World* by M. Takeo Magruder, D. Baker and D. Steele.

[4] Cf. *Web3Dart* (www.web3dart.org), a series of international exhibitions (1998-2007) showcasing the best 3D artwork on the Web.

[5] When all individuals contribute as equal members of a group and share ownership (in terms of intellectual property rights and copyright) of the final output. Cf. Boddington, 2006.

[6] The term, coined by Neil Stephenson in his novel *Snow Crash* (1992), refers to an immersive 3D virtual realm that is metaphorically based upon the real world.

[7] www.turbulence.org/Works/vitruvianworld/

[8] King's Visualisation Lab (www.kvl.cch.kcl.ac.uk/) is based in the Centre for Computing in the Humanities, King's College London.

[9] Cf. Morgan, 1914 and Smith, 2003.

[10] The term for end-user modification of a computer program or device.

[11] Cf. Magruder, 2007.

[12] Conceived by Dr. Hugh Denard (Associate-Director of King's Visualisation Lab) and funded by the Eduserv Foundation, the *Theatron 3* project reconstructed twenty historic theatre sites within *Second Life* for research, education and virtual performance.

[13] Short for primitive object, the term for the basic geometric building unit in *Second Life*.

[14] A 'corporeal space' that is animated by the body. Cf. Appia, 1921 in Beacham, 1993.

[15] Short for simulator, the term for *Second Life's* primary unit of land consisting of $256m^2$ of virtual space.

[16] The primary control device for the *Wii* (Nintendo's 7th generation games console) containing a three-axis accelerometer and infrared optical sensors for tracking, and wireless connectivity via *Bluetooth*.

[17] www.opensimulator.org

CHAPTER FIVE

DEVELOPING MOVING IMAGES FOR THE MULTIMEDIA PERFORMANCE 'FROM ANGER TO SADNESS' – REPRESENTATION, INTERPRETATION AND PERCEPTION

FRANK MILLWARD

1. Introduction

The Visual Voice (www.thevisualvoice.co.uk) is an ongoing collaborative research project involving Dr Frank Millward and Dr John Rubin. The work seeks to represent the attributes of emotive vocal utterances as abstracted 3D moving images and to theorise and understand how we interpret complex emotive interactive exchanges between human and machine, sound and image, vocal quality and perceived emotive intent.

When I began this work it soon became apparent that my interests were located across a number of fields of study - Psychology of Emotion, Voice Science, Physiology and the Acoustics of Singing, Affective & Interactive Computing, Sonic Art and a variety of fields involving Digital Media. Early investigations pointed towards an interdisciplinary approach that made connections between empirical, qualitative and practice-led evidence about audiovisual representations of emotive vocal utterances.

With this in mind I sought to combine a scientific with practice-led research approach. I would negotiate a direction that explored the empirical with the artistic - the pragmatic with the intuitive - listening / hearing with seeing / feeling - analytical with instinctive - design with chaos - da Vinci with Dali - Kandinsky with Darwin - Ligeti with Marclay - reflexive practice with linear scientific logic - where testing ideas using interactive processes is incorporated into developing a line of investigation that has a range of media and performative outcomes.

Through the development of moving images for the piece, *'From Anger To Sadness'*[1] I have begun to address issues involving the interpretation and perception of represented emotive vocal utterances in a multimedia performance context. My discussion here will focus on the development of nasendoscopy[2] and spectrographic images[3].

2. "From Anger To Sadness"

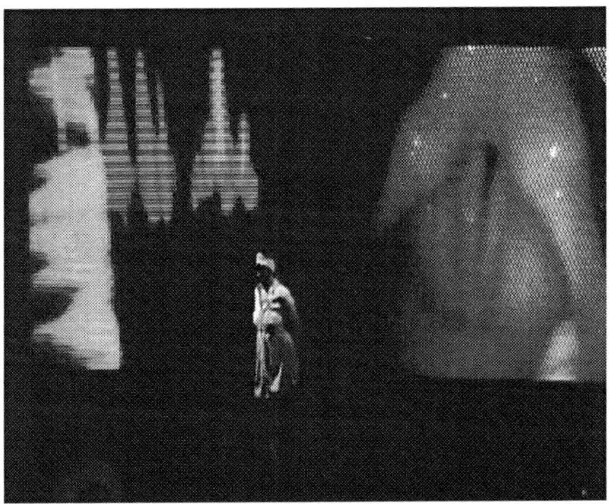

Figure 1 Performance of 'From Anger To Sadness' - Projected spectrographic and nasendoscopy images

The basis emotive states of Fear - Shock - Denial - Hope - Anger and Sadness were used to structure the interactive emotive journey, 'From Anger to Sadness'. The performance presents a blindfolded performer[4] flanked by two screens - screen one (Fig 1 - left) projects spectrographic analysis moving images of the live sound of the voice of the performer and screen two (Fig 1 - right) projects a pre-recorded video which includes nasendoscopy imaging of the vocal folds performing acted emotive utterances using variable vowel expressions of the basic emotions described. An enactive relationship is established between the performer and the spectrographic imaging (screen one) in performance. A reactive relationship is established with screen two, which presents a video that combines shot footage with nasendoscopy images prerecorded by the same performer, soprano, Heather Keens.

3. Emotive Utterance - Nasendoscopy and Spectrographic Imaging

Developing this work began with observations made while viewing nasendoscopy footage of the vocal folds of a singer with voice damage. I noticed a connection between the vocal sound and the moving vocal fold imagery - there was a strong phonaesthetic synchronicity. Nasendoscopy images generate a wide variety of emotive responses including fascination - disgust - shock - curiosity - wonder - along with intuitive responses involving the conflicting dilemma of simultaneous attraction and repulsion. Such observations led to the decision to record a variety of variable vowel expressions of both sung and speech qualities of acted emotive vocal utterances. With my colleague, Dr John Rubin we agreed upon a methodological approach, the main focus of which was to use an endoscope to film the vocal folds of a performer while engaged in the delivery of acted emotive vocal utterances and to use these moving images in a performance context as representations of emotive states. Dr Rubin supervised these nasendoscopy recordings in his surgery. The sessions yielded approximately nine minutes of moving image materials.

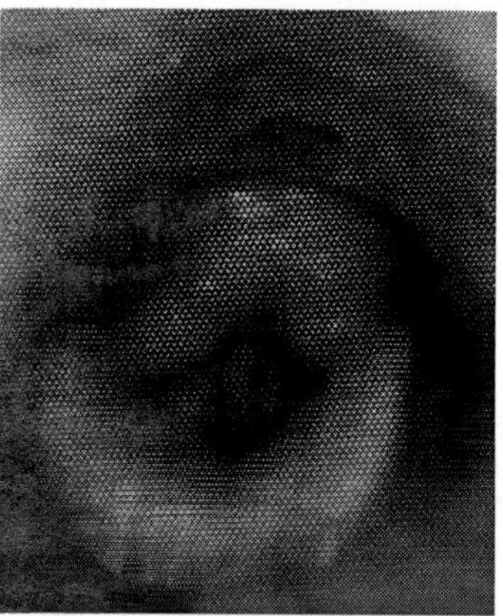

Figure 2 Nasendoscopy still - opera quality sung ‘e’ vowel

My interest in pursuing this method was motivated by the intimate power of the moving vocal fold imagery to communicate something beyond the literality of its apparent function. Viewing nasendoscopy images produces a significant emotive response in the spectator. The perceptive experience presents the combination of hearing an emotive sound quality while seeing the vocal folds moving in the production of those emotive sounds.

Further explorations led me to a detailed investigations concerning the variety of possible sound qualities that can be produced in the limited sonic bandwidth of a voice - spoken and sung qualities such as: creak - breath tone - siren - sigh - belt - twang - cry - opera and so on. As a musician I was familiar with reading the spectrographic images of sound files - time - frequency - amplitude - texture - envelope - contour and so on.

Translating vocal qualities through the analysis of a moving spectrographic image became the starting point for the idea of producing a 3D moving image of an utterance as an abstract emotive visual expression - to develop an emotively intuitive spectrograph - the idea that the spectrograph could have an aesthetic that reflected emotive qualities. What would a sad 'sigh' look like as a sculptured spectrographic type object? What sort of space would it occupy? How might its shape, colour, texture represent its emotive intent? The following spectrographic image (Fig 3) is a reading of an acted 'distress' utterance of an 'o' vowel. The presence of 'creak'[5] quality can be seen by the way the image is formed as a succession of interrupted segments - the continuation of colour is regularly interrupted by the absence of colour.

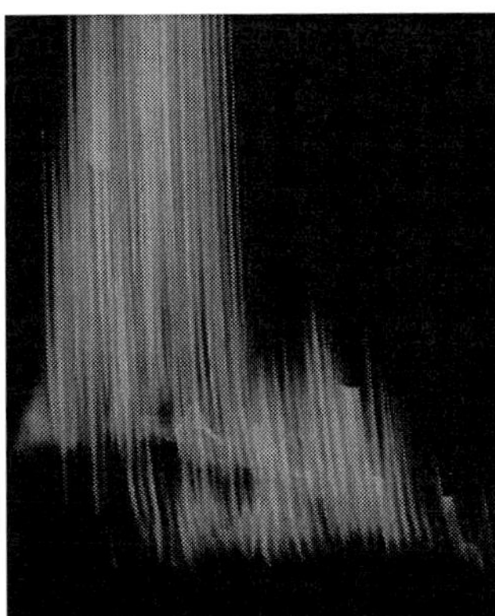

Figure 3 Spectrographic still - distressful utterance of an 'o' vowel with creak quality

4. The Sonic Components of an Emotive Utterance

Within the field of emotional psychology, work involving emotive vocal expression is a fast growing area of study. Of particular note are the writings of K. Scherer et al at the University of Geneva and R. Cowie et al at Queens University Belfast[6]. Among other topics these teams have produced a body of work about the expression and interactive nature of the voice and emotion. In the context of the vocal communication of emotion, Scherer describes four main areas of acoustic measures in emotional speech:

> time-related measures, intensity related measures, measures related to fundamental frequency, and more complicated time-frequency-energy measures. The first three categories are linked mainly to the perceptual dimensions of speech rate, loudness and pitch respectively and the fourth category has more to do with perceived timbre and voice quality[7]

When exploring these measures as possible representational components of emotive utterances, parallels can be noted between the sonic and the visual such as:

	SONIC	VISUAL
Time-related measures	Tempo - pulse	Rhythm - cut or editing style
	Audio panning - surround or stereo positioning in the sonic field	Camera motion or tracking - near / far - left / right - moving / still
	Direction - sounds moves to or away from the horizon / vanishing point - left / right	Shape - perspective / flat 2D / 3D / distorted or abstract framing
Intensity related measures	Timbre - sonic texture	Colouration
	Amplitude	Lucidity
Measures related to fundamental frequency	Pitch - tessitura - high /low / left / right / sonic contours / modalities of pitch / modalities of noise or ambience	Frame positioning - near / far / left / right / modalities of framing / modalities of image texture or contrast

Time-frequency-energy measures	Acoustic envelope	Time related colour transformations
	Intonation contour - sonic equalisation or compression schema	Terrain or topological schema - visual landscape navigation
	Sonic with visual panning motion	Focus motion - colour evolution

Maitland Graves (1951) points out similarities in sonic and visual art design concepts[8].

- elements of design - line - direction - shape - size - texture - proportion - value - colour
- principles of design - repetition - alternation - harmony - graduation - contrast, opposition or conflict - unity - balance

5. The Performance of Discrete Emotions

Considering the parallel representational aspects above regarding the combined visual and sonic experience of viewing nasendoscopy moving images, questions arise which confront issues that lie at the heart of understandings about audiovisual representational language and the interpretation of the relationships between sound, moving image and emotive intent. Take for example the quivering vocal sound of 'fear' - the moving vocal folds do not have complete closure - the folds shake or quiver - there is a visual onomatopoeia - a phonaesthesia - the quivering sound is mirrored in the moving image of the quivering folds.

This you might think is not unusual and to be expected - physiologically the body can shake with fear however, it may be shaking with cold or with anticipation. How would we know the difference? Is it possible to know the difference if we were to just hear the sound or just see the moving image? Certain basic assumptions can be drawn to describe aspects that parallel the behaviour of the sound and the behaviour of the vocal folds involved in the production of that emotive sound.

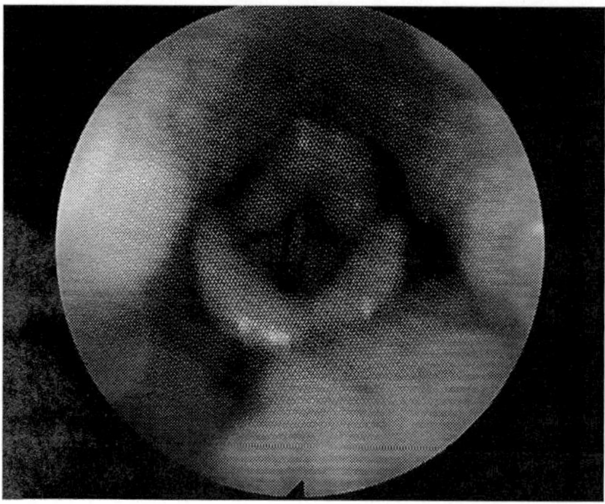

Figure 4 Fear

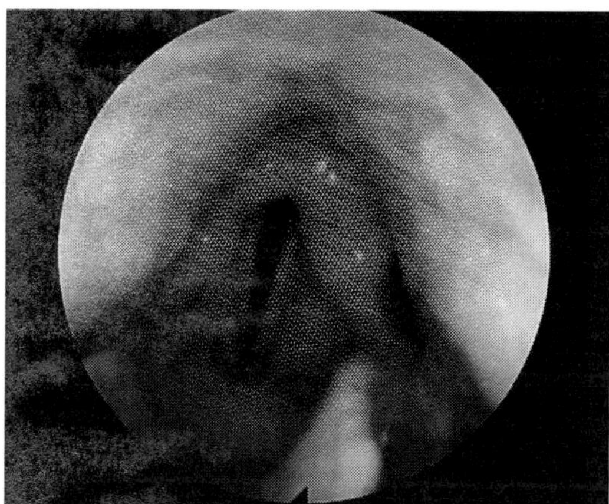

Figure 5 'Sad Sigh'

Consider the issue of contour. The sound of a 'sad sigh' (Fig 5) has a contour envelope which starts with a tone that falls away (glissandos) to an airy breathy sound - there is a downward inflection - for the production of that sound the vocal folds have closure, then visibly decelerate in velocity, the larynx widens and the musculature relaxes - a restrained 'cry' quality. Visually and sonically there are parallels - the moving image of the folds look like they sound. This poses an important question - if we see the image of the folds without hearing the sound do we perceive or interpret the moving image as having a sad quality?

Michel Chion in his book *Audio-Vision - Sound on Screen* discusses ways in which sound 'renders the perception of time in image…'. The fact that a sound is a vibration - implies movement through time, one could also argue direction - dependant on tempo, pitch and textural modulations. There are few examples of a 'still' sound - even a sixty-cycle power hum, which appears to sound static, can have perceptible modulations. While sound generally pre-supposes movement, a moving image however, can contain things in the frame that may remain fixed or 'still'. Viewing the vocal folds in the production of an emotive utterance I would suggest is a model of phonaesthetic synchronicity. What you see - the movement of the folds and the larynx - is mirrored in what you hear. Issues to do with temporality such as envelope, contour or '*time-frequency-energy measures*' (Scherer 2003) work in favor of the literal visual representation of the emotive utterance - there is limited processing placed on the sound by the articulators as the greater part of an utterance happens in the region of the folds.

Through observing the vocal folds in emotive phonation I have noticed visual and sonic representational models of *time-frequency-energy* that actually or metaphorically transpose to a variety of media. A 'sad sigh' mirrored in the slow fade to black of a doleful filmic transition, a decrescendo, a diminuendo - the envelope shapes and contours of musical phrasing is perhaps the most obvious place to find examples - cadence, perfect end or interrupted unresolved inflections can all be observed in the vocal fold activity of emotive utterances motivated by feelings of denial and hope.

Sonically, rhythmic knowledge, learned from emotive vocal response (primitive emotions of sex, fear, anger) are embed into our emotional memories[9]. Such rhythms have evolved and developed through representations that use pulse and tempo enacted in a variety of ritualistic forms - fast excited - slow sad and so on. I would argue that emotionally motivated vocal fold motion is an ideal model for the representation of the correlates between moving image and associated sound.

As you might expect, the principal driving element, the breath, determines phrase and models many of the ways we interpret and relate to narrative time-based enactments. Perhaps this is a clue as to why abstract visual art is more acceptable to the eye than abstract music to the ear - the intellectually devised musical language of 'anti-pulse' rhythm (found in experimental western art music) is less familiar to our primitive emotive knowledge bank than the visual language of the 'sign' which taps more comfortably and directly into that same primitive embedded knowledge[10].

6. Representation, Interpretation and Perception

The idea of representing an emotive utterance as a moving image that is perceived and / or interpreted as communicating that emotive state led to the development of a number of fundamental pertinent research questions - including:

Can moving imagery derived from the sonic attributes of an emotive utterance be perceived and / or interpreted to communicate the emotive intent of that utterance?

If we hear an utterance such as a 'sigh', without seeing who made that sound, what is it that makes it possible to understand what we are hearing? How do we know if the 'sigh' is an expression of sadness, frustration, tiredness or something else?[11]

If along with the sound we see the face of the person making that 'sigh', or if we see moving vocal folds in the act of making that 'sigh', or a moving image representing that 'sigh', how does the visual reference influence our perception or interpretation of the emotion expressed? What is the relationship between sound and moving image when the relationship between these elements is perceived to work in synchronization? If sound and image are perceived to be oppositional? e.g. a sad sigh with a smile - a laugh with an angry face. Understanding the relationships between sound, moving image and emotive intent must be considered as central to solving the problem of producing a moving image that without hearing the sound that produced it, communicates emotional intent.

A multimodal approach involving facial, vocal, gesture and physiological factors, gives perhaps the best and most comprehensive way of representing or interpreting human emotive intent because there is a perceived visual confirmation that reinforces the sonic signal. Other problems present because of the subjective nature of the experience of emotion (Schroder, 2003) - is the emotion acted or real - mixed or single emotive expression - is it the emotive state of the 'vocaliser' or is the emotive utterance being used as a 'tool of social influence on listener sensitivities?' (Bachorowski / Owren, 2003)?

Such issues raise questions about a 'science describing sounds, joined to an art of hearing them' (Schaffer, 1966) or in this case - of representing a sound, joined to an art of seeing them.

> "Wolfgang Kohler's pioneering psychological experiment from 1927, in which he asked subjects, 'which of the figures below represent the sound *maluma*, and which one represents the sound *takete*?'" [12]

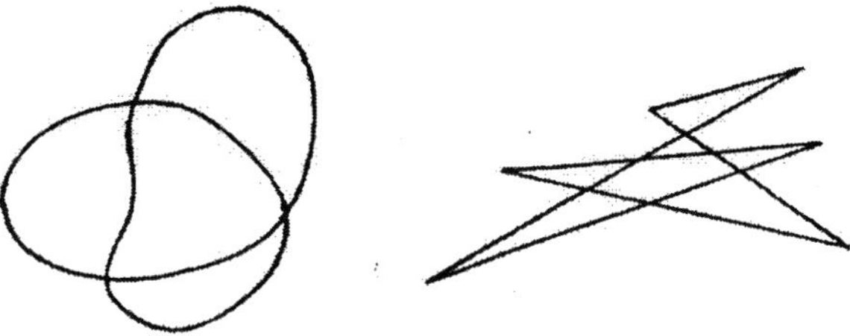

Figure 6 Maluma - Takete

Nearly all viewers respond with the same answer - (maluma - left image - takete - right image). This still image example offers a choice of assignment between image and possible sound. Interpreting this phonaesthetic relationship relating image and sound is to some extent instinctive or learned - as described above - elements are embedded in our emotional memories.

The sound of the word 'maluma' is voiced with an open resonating sound - this is because of the modulation envelope occurring when voicing 'ma - lu - ma' - the presence of the back vowel sounds 'a' - (ah) and 'u' - (ooh) producing an open fluid rounded (lower) sound than 'ta - ke - te' - which is voiced with a forward vowel sound that has brighter higher partials 'a' - (ah) 'e' - (e) - low rounded open, as opposed to higher sharper sound. The voicing of the sound parallels the visible shapes - audio and visual embedded memories are triggered to deduce the identification of the most probable pairing.

The work 'Messa di Voce' by Gollan Levin (2004) uses these ideas to develop some very engaging real-time imagery where 'software transforms every vocal nuance into correspondingly complex, subtly differentiated and highly expressive graphics'. Similar ideas are used in works such as 'Split Splat' by Nagalingam, Anthopoulos and Al Hashimi (Al Hashimi 2006) and interactive games such as 'Ghost in the Cave' (Rinman et al. 2003) and 'Sing Pong' - a projected game 'based on the use of paralinguistic characteristics of voice to control the traditional video game *Pong'* (Al Hashimi 2006).

Figure 7 'Anger'

In 'From Anger to Sadness', the emotive states are represented as a series of mediated moving images - the spectrographic moving image - screen one - left hand side - green shapes - graphically represent anger. The moving image is produced in real-time through a microphone connected to the voice of the performer. The image is manipulated and colour processed in real time with the vocal performance[13]. Screen two projects an accompanying video - right hand side - of pre-recorded nasendoscopy images of acted 'angry' utterances.

Emotive utterances represented simultaneously as spectrographic and nasendoscopy imaging in combination with a live performance has a multimodal impact that triggers various types of emotive recognitions and responses - 'it reminds me of …' (memory recognition) - 'it makes me feel …' (emotive response) - 'it reminds me of …and then I feel…' (recognition / response). At this stage of the development of this work I have focused on spectator response in terms of these basic types of interpretation - memory recognition - emotive response - recognition / response.

The energy transmitted in the portrayal of anger in performance often elicited the response of fear. Some spectators were frightened to be in the presence of live vocalised 'angry' utterances - it created a tense atmosphere - the unpredictability of an angry energy often projecting a sense of danger which was responded to with the feeling of fear - (recognition / response). To expand upon an idea expressed above - is it the 'spectator' or is the emotive signifier being used as a 'tool of social influence?' Representation has both a 'transmission' and a 'reception' component. For example 'fear' might be depicted by something that represents the idea of fear (a sign) or might be depicted as something which creates a sense of fear. Emotive 'transmission' is made without being able to predict how it is to be received - issues here involve empathy or emotional intelligence (recognition / response). Sadness, for example, consistently attracts an empathetic response - the spectator is often willing to feel or share in the feeling of the pain of sadness (acted) with the performer.

Figure 8 'Sadness'

Perhaps this is understandable when considering the above image (Fig 8) from the accompanying video - a close-up of tearful eyes - a traditional clichéd signifier, which is more likely to elicit an empathetic emotive response than an abstract image or an image of moving vocal folds.

7. Future Directions

The intention is to continue to develop multimedia performances of this type, using the audiovisual documentations to make further interactive multimedia experiences that test and identify spectator reactions in emotive terms. These reactions will be collected and made to form a database of identified emotive utterances.

Vocal analysis and medical instrumentation and imaging techniques can now make appropriate measurements of relevant sonic vocal qualities, such as fundamental frequency (pitch), physiological measurements, position of the tongue and vocal fold vibration and so on that can be used to inform the development of algorithms that could express these qualities as 3D moving images. The moving images could thus represent the emotively identified utterances as a vision of visual emotive vocal expression.

Interactive multimedia performance testing establishes a research mechanism for the simultaneous accumulation of database materials and the gathering of evidence about the nature of emotive utterances, where representation, perception and interpretation can be analysed and evaluated through an ongoing interactive process, the testing process itself being experimented with, refined and improved throughout various phases of the project.

Throughout, ideas are developed for improving the ways in which spectator engagement is negotiated. Current work is focusing on two emotive states - denial and hope - with a view to gathering responses about how visually represented emotive utterances are perceived to communicate these emotive intents.

References

Al Hashimi S. "Users as performers in vocal interactive media: The role of expressive voice visualization". International Journal of Performance Arts and Digital Media 2:3, (2006): 275-295.

Bachorowski J.A. and Orwen M.J. "Sounds of Emotion: Production and Perception of Affect-Related Vocal Acoustics". Annals of the New York Academy of Science (2003): 244-265.

Chion M. *Audio - Vision: Sound on Screen.* New York: Columbia University Press, 1994.

Darwin C. *The Expression of the Emotions in Man and Animals.* London: John Murray, 1872.

Graves M. *The Art of Color and Design.* New York: McGraw-Hill, 1951.

Johnstone T. and Scherer K.R. "Vocal Expression of Emotion". In *The Handbook of Emotion* ed. M. Lewis & J. Haviland. New York: Guildford, (2000): 224-225.

Kohler W. *Gestalt Psychology.* New York: Liveright, 1947.

Lavin G. & Liberman Z. "*In Situ* Visualization in Real-Time Interactive Installation and Performance" paper delivered at The 3rd International Symposium on Non-Photorealistic Animation and Rendering, Annecy, France (2004) available at *http://www.tmema.org/messa/messa.html*

Lyons A. D. "Time Space Texture: An Approach to Audio-Visual Composition". PhD diss., University of Sydney, 2003.

Rinman M., Friberg A., Bendiksen B., Kjellmo I., Cirotteau D., McCarthy H., Mazzarino B. and Dahl S. *Ghost in the Cave: An Interactive Collaborative Game Using Non-Verbal Communication'* in R. Bresin (ed.), Proceedings of SMAC03, Vol II. (2003): 561-563

Schroder M. "Experimental study of affect bursts". *Speech Communication,* Vol 40 (2003): 99-116.

Schaeffer, P. *Traité des Objets Musicaux.* Paris: Editions du Seuil, 1966.

Scherer K.R. "Vocal communication of emotion: A review of research paradigms". *Speech Communication,* Vol 40. (2003): 227–256.

Taylor S.F., Liberzon I., Fig L.M., Decker L.R., Minoshima S., Koeppe R.A., "The Effect of Emotional Content on Visual Recognition Memory: A PET Activation Study". *NeuroImage*, Vol 8, (1998): 188-197.

Wertheimer M. "Laws of Organization in Perceptual Forms". (1923) Translation published in Ellis, W. *A source book of Gestalt psychology.* London: Routledge & Kegan Paul. (1938): 71-88.

Websites

Cowie R. - Humaine - Research on Emotions and Human-Machine Interaction *http://emotion-research.net/* Queen's University Belfast (accessed 12th April 2009)

Lavin G. & Liberman Z. (2003) 'Messa di Voce: An Audiovisual Performance and Installation for Voice and Interactive Media' http://www.tmema.org/messa/messa.html (accessed 6th April 2009)

National Review of Live Art Produced by New Moves International http://www.newmoves.co.uk/nrla-2009/57-archive-2009-nrla/496-frank-millward (accessed 8th May 2009)

Schill B. Spectrographic Analysis for the EVP Researcher http://www.iprfinc.com/images/technique/spectroanal.html (accessed 8th April 2009)

Notes

[1] Performed at the National Review of Live Art - Feb 09 http://www.newmoves.co.uk/nrla-2009/57-archive-2009-nrla/496-frank-millward

[2] moving images gathered by inserting a camera through the nose to video the vocal folds in action

[3] a visual analysis of the sonic spectrum to visually demonstrate its composition and motion

[4] the blindfold is used to concentrate the focus of the performer entirely on reactive / interactive listening

[5] 'creak' is characterized by a low frequency vibration in the vocal folds - periodicity is disturbed

[6] R. Cowie - Humaine - Research on Emotions and Human-Machine Interaction http://emotion-research.net/

[7] T. Johnstone & K.R. Scherer (2000)

[8] discussed in *Time Space Texture: An Approach to Audio-Visual Composition* - PhD Thesis by Andrew D. Lyons. University of Sydney (2003)

[9] many of these models serve as design templates for software program commands and / or special effects algorithms e.g. noise across an image

[10] the focus of yet another discussion

[11] this relates to the Pierre Schaeffer (1966) idea about *acousmatic* sound - the sound we hear without seeing the cause of that sound

[12] Kohler W. (1947)

[13] using MAX/MSP Jitter as the interpretative vehicle that transforms sound into processed 3D moving images - mixed, manipulated and processed in this performance by Fleeta Chew Siegel

CHAPTER SIX

RISK, INTIMACY, AND PERFORMATIVITY IN VIRTUAL WORLDS

LISA NEWMAN

> As long as it lives, love hovers on the brink of defeat. It dissolves its past as it goes; it leaves no fortified trenches behind to which it could retreat, running for shelter in the case of trouble. And it knows not what lies ahead and what the future may bring. . . Love is a mortgage loan drawn on an uncertain and inscrutable future.
> —Zygmunt Bauman

The goal of this paper is to discuss the formation of social and intimate bonds in virtual, on-line worlds such as Second Life, and the role of performance to continue to act as a lens to emphasize, question, and challenge these new developments in societal behaviors and mores. Of particular interest is where the lines between fiction and reality, on-line and off-line, blur and distort due to the lack of distinction between virtual identities - "avatars" - and real world lives.

This essay is a segment of a much larger thesis exploration of ways of loving in Western cultures, and how performance art has exposed forms of intimacy and partnership which have been hidden, silenced, or forbidden during the last several decades. During the early onset of the AIDS epidemic in the 1980's, for example, artists like Ron Athey, Tim Miller, and Diamanda Galas risked censorship and persecution for creating public presentations that showed the loss, the risk, and the love within the lives of those affected.

The paper is divided into two sections. In the first half, I will give examples of current trends in on-line intimate relationships, along with socio-psychological theories pertaining to the search for intimacy and love in the virtual age of the new millennium. In the second half, I will be examining the potential for performance artists to continue to present challenging physical work in an on-line arena where their bodies are replaced by on-line avatars. Throughout the paper I seek answers to the questions: How and why do we communicate intimacy and love and form lasting bonds through on-line networks and virtual avatars? Is there as much at risk within the love of the deathless avatar as there is between mortal, physical bodies? What is the future of the physical body in love? What is the future role of the performance artist in the virtual world?

I: Love and the Avatar

Sociologist Zygmunt Bauman describes late twentieth-century Western culture as a 'liquid' culture, or an occurrence in a consumer-based society in which bonds between couples are fluid, and life-long commitment to another is no longer a goal, as it was for past generations:

> Connections are 'virtual relations'. Unlike old-fashioned relationships (not to mention 'committed' relationships, let alone long-term commitments), they seem to be made to the measure of a liquid life setting where 'romantic possibilities' (and not only 'romantic' ones) are supposed and hoped to come and go with ever greater speed and in ever thinning crowds... Unlike 'real relationships', 'virtual relationships' are easy to enter and to exit...you can always press 'delete'. (Bauman 2003, xii)

Bauman continues to discuss the idea that networks have replaced binary, committed relationships, wherein one's desire for companionship can be fragmented, and spread out over a web of relationships with numerous possibilities. If one relationship ends, the web is still held up by several other bonds to fill the void left by the one. Bauman posits that love is like any other commodity; like investing in the stock market. The more you spread around your wealth, the less likely you are to lose it all in one unfortunate, risky venture. On-line networking tools like Facebook, Friendster, and MySpace make it possible for these webs of friends and loved ones to be formed and maintained easily and frequently.

But what happens when the web of on-line casual networking expands to include real world intimate relationships? A recent study at the University of Guelph has found a connection betweek Facebook usage and jealousy and suspicion in romantic and sexual relationships. Amy Muisc, a PhD student in psychology, who conducted the study with student colleague Emily Christofides, surveyed 308 Facebook users who were asked about their personal relationships, demographics and the amount of time they spent on Facebook. They discovered that most of the participants were aware that exposing personal information on the site increased the chance of inciting feelings of jealousy, and that the temptation to monitor their partner's Facebook activity was “too hard to resist.” "It fosters a vicious cycle," Christofides said. "If one partner in a relationship discloses personal information, it increases the likelihood that the other person will do the same, which increases the likelihood of jealousy." (University of Guelph 2009)

In Facebook, privacy is often difficult to control as the goal is to be able to access friends of friends in order to invite them to join your own network. This 'harvesting' of friends can be done without the host's knowledge, and messaging between people is often exposed on public 'walls'. This new kind of pseudo-omnipresence makes fidelity within relationships a challenging venture. As Guelph psychology professor, Serge Desmaris, describes: "In the past, people in romantic or sexual relationships were not, for the most part, subjected to daily scrutiny of their social exchanges by their partner," he said. "But this is the new reality for some; aspects of their lives that were once private are now open for all to see." (University of Guelph 2009)

In recent news, this public accessibility of the private in on-line worlds has resulted in very unusual crimes of passion. In Japan, a woman's “sudden divorce from her online husband in a virtual game world made her so angry that she logged on [as him] and killed his digital persona”. Jailed with “suspicion of illegally accessing a computer and manipulating electronic data”, she may face up to five years in prison and $5000 in fines. The marriage between the two only existed within the game “Maple Story”, (a virtual world similar to Second Life). They lived 690 miles away from each other in Japan and never met in person outside of the game. (Yamaguchi 2008)

In England, a couple who met and wed on Second Life before wedding in real life filed for divorce after one found the other's avatar in an act of infidelity in the virtual world. In another instance, a truck driver was sentenced to 14 years in prison for the murder of his estranged wife who he killed after he found out she changed her Facebook status to "single" only days after they split up. (Satter 2008)

The intent of virtual on-line worlds like Second Life and Maple Story seems to hover somewhere between a networking tool and a fantasy role-playing game. Like Facebook, they offer opportunities to make connections with other like-minded people around common interests, but unlike Facebook, where members are encouraged to use actual photos of themselves along with true identities, Second Life allows for the construction and actualization of a myriad of game-like fantasies with shifting identities and visual representations of one's self through the creation of avatars.

I would posit this feature is what confuses the borders between fantasy and reality in the formation of on-line intimate relationships. In the virtual world, behaviors can be explored without any repercussions or lasting ramifications, but the effect of watching one's avatar engage in actions which would be considered to be amoral or illegal in real life must leave some emotional and psychological residue in the player. In his essay, *Blended Realities* Matt Daly elaborates on this theory:

> . . .It's sometimes within the context of a game, loosened from repercussion and judgement, (sic) that the user/audience member can engage experimentally with others, and with his/her own personality. 'Emergent gameplay' describes the unpredictable changes in the dynamics of personae, ideology, behavior, and so forth, within the game environment. It is thought to be the result of this state of relaxed levity that allows the player to experiment with new modes of behaviors and ideas that'd be harder to act out in real life. (Daly 2008)

Physical risk in virtual relationships is often more symbolic that actual, as avatars may be deleted and resurrected by the user in its precise form, or, if the user desires, as an entirely new body with a different gender, age, race, or even species. Though users conceptually understand that behind each avatar is a live human, what is experienced directly is the icon for whatever identity the user would like to present publicly, rather than a true self. The loss of an icon may not always be equated with the loss of a life, and risky behavior may be explored with a more cavalier approach in a digital world of icons than in the flesh-and-blood world, though occasionally with irreversible consequences as the virtual world bleeds into the real.

On October 16, 2006, a teenage girl, Megan Meier, hung herself because the boy who she had fallen in love with through the on-line network, MySpace, had sent her a message which read: "the world would be a better place without you." What Meier never learned was that the boy was fictitious. The MySpace profile was created by a mother-daughter team who planned to use the imaginary boy to seduce Meier and find out whether Meier was spreading rumors about the daughter. The mother has been charged not with murder, but 'cyberbullying', and a violation of the MySpace code of conduct, which forbids on-line harassment. (Watkins 2008).

Perhaps the real world crimes listed above are evidence of the desire of the users to *validate* the reality of their on-line love by creating finalities in the real world which ensure that whatever the outcome of the relationship, the love was *real,* and not a digital simulation.

Jean Baudrillard, in *Simulacra and Simulations*, describes the anguish experienced by Iconoclasts in their goal to erase the images of God in order to preserve the true essence of God, and eliminate what they felt were false representations of the deity and their belief system:

> Their [Iconoclasts] rage to destroy images rose precisely because they sensed this omnipotence of simulacra, this facility they have of erasing God from the consciousnesses of people, and the overwhelming, destructive truth which they suggest: that ultimately there has never been any God; that only simulacra exist; indeed that God himself has only ever been his own simulacrum. . . One can live with the idea of a distorted truth. But their metaphysical despair came from the idea that the images concealed nothing at all, and that in fact they were not images, such as the original model would have made them, but actually perfect simulacra forever radiant with their own fascination. (Baudrillard 1988, 168)

For a lover to become enraptured with the simulacra "forever radiant with their own fascination", as in the case of the on-line avatar, the risk lies in the possibility that the images of the loved one may, in fact, "conceal nothing at all" (Baudrillard 1988, 168).

In this essay about love within virtual worlds, I feel it is crucial to look once again to performance art as an indicator of how we will progress culturally when dealing with love and intimacy in the age of the on-line avatar.

The performance and 'body art' of the late 1960's and 1970's was created, in part, with the intention of eliminating the use of art as mere objective representation, and instead to use it to explore truth through direct physical actions. In a slight rewording of the Bertolt Brecht quote, Northern Irish artist Andre Stitt writes, "Art is not a mirror, it is a fucking hammer" (Stitt 2001). By this, Stitt means that art, and perfomance in particular, is not designed to merely reflect what already exists, but to challenge existing norms. Performance work is often autobiographical in nature, and there is an ownership of identity rather than the creation of a theatrical character. There is little or no separation between the artist, their body, and their message – thus creating the risk of emotional and psychological exposure, of physical harm, and personal freedom of expression through censorship. As Linda Montano, an artist known for creating multi-year long performances, explains, "Our bodies are our matter, our raw material. . ." (Montano 2000, xiii)

In this next section, I will be comparing the reactions of audiences, or users, to the live work of Marina Abramovic and Ulay in the 1970's, with the recreation of this work in the virtual world of Second Life in 2007, and discuss the potentials for future translations of physical expression through performative actions as technologies progress.

II. Performing intimacy in virtual worlds

In a recent article by Rachel Wolff in *ARTnews* magazine, she reported the work of collaborative duo, Eva and Franco Mattes, who, as part of Performa07, recreated famous performative works which explore intimate behaviors through their animated avatars in Second Life, including Marina Abramovic and Ulay's *Imponderabilia*(1977) which was performed by the Mattes' avatars in front of both live and virtual audiences. Participants squeezed through the narrow doorway to the gallery, originally flanked by Abramovic and Ulay's naked bodies, but this time, the virtual audience took risks with the Mattes' avatars which did not occur in the original event.

In the original 1977 performance, participants were surprised to find their own live images staring back at them from television screens as they were filmed squeezing through the gate of Abramovic and Ulay, and forming a spontaneous menage-a-trois. In the 2007 Mattes recreation, some of the patrons "stripped down, too; one seemed to be getting fresh with avatar Eva, displaying the heightened expressiveness typical of the virtual realm." (Wolff 2008)

In an excerpt of interview posted on their website, the Mattes' explain that "the performer and her audience only interact thorough their avatars:

everything is mediated, nothing is spontaneous. More or less the opposite of what performance art is supposed to be." The apprehension, discomfort, or titillation of Abramovic and Ulay's audience was notably absent from the Mattes' performance, partially due to the shortcomings of the current available technology. Thus, the Mattes' performance was merely iconic, whereas the 1977 performance created a social experiment regarding intimacy.

I interpret the goal of the Mattes' performances to be an exploration of the potential for simulated human interactions in virtual worlds, and they chose the media of performance art specifically because of its inherent liveness and immediacy within modes of artistic communication. When asked why they chose to recreate pieces like *Imponderabilia,* and Vito Acconci's *Seedbed*, (in which Acconci masturbated beneath a gallery floor, amplifying his voice and breathing to the audience above), they said that they were interested in performances which were particularly "paradoxical" when performed in a virtual world, due to the importance of the actual physicality of the artists' fleshy bodies in the original presentations. (Mattes 2008)

There is a lack of an exclusive first person experience for a virtual audience, as Second Life allows the participants to vacillate between an omnipotent, third-person view as well as through the eyes of their avatar. They can be, in a sense, their own audience – able to watch themselves interacting with the artists and the other audience members. Following this logic, they are also their own voyeurs and judges in a way that exceeds the parental voice and instead becomes almost god-like. Watching one's avatar create an act of violence, or heroism, or love-making in a virtual world translates into a sense of power in the avatar's creator that may not exist for them in real life.

But what if the disparity of "realness" in virtual worlds is remedied as new technologies are rapidly being developed and perfected? When the ability to fully actualize the experience of pressing up between two naked bodies in a virtual world completely mirrors the experience of a live, real-life performance on a psychological and fully sensory level – what will happen to the relevance of the body within performance and live art?

What would happen if contemporary body artists were to recreate their challenging performances through avatars in public on-line worlds, such as Second Life? Take the example of Ron Athey, who gained notoriety in the 1980's when he created a live action involving using his own HIV+ blood to make prints, and then hung the prints over the audience. Though the risk of infection from the blood was minimal for the audience, the piece was a comment on the social fear surrounding the AIDS virus at the time, and resulted in panic amongst the participants. Though twenty years later more is known about the virus, the fear of infection still exists within the cultural ethos.

Though viruses exist in the on-line world as well – often eradicating programs and computer functions as they would destroy immune systems in bodies – they have not, as of yet, killed in 'real-life'. If Athey were to exist as an avatar in the world of Second Life, how would an avatar-audience react? If the audience were to be given information about the artist's life in the physical world - would the same fear of infection remain if one's avatar came into close proximity to Athey's virtual blood? What if the audience was told that the image of Athey's avatar was embedded with a computer virus, programmed to infect and destroy avatars in a simulation of the contagion in the real world? Would this result in avatars developing and practicing safe sex in on-line relationships? Would this translate into real-life decisions surrounding the care and protection of oneself and others back in the physical world?

Performance theorist and practitioner, Lois Keidan, posits that the performance and Live Art of the late 1990s "has proved that it is uniquely positioned to articulate and represent seemingly problematic issues through alternative strategies, and that it is one of the most flexible and responsive artistic tools there is to pursue new ways of representing and responding to these shifting and uncertain times." (Keidan 1988, 3)

When our identities are constantly in flux, how does one establish social bonds in a state of unpredictability? Perhaps, as Keidan suggested, it is the *flexibility* of the live performance that positions it as a crucial and successful mode of communication for a society with fluid identities, a rapidly changing environment which is dissolving as a result of our need to consume and replace, and the growing number of virtual romances replacing physical meetings.

I would posit that the role of the performance artist within the ever-expanding virtual world will be to remind us of the tenuousness nature of physical, emotional, and psychological limitations, as well as to create a lens to continue to explore our desires for intimacy and companionship.

Several recent projects have already shown that the desire of the user to experience real-world ritual around loss in virtual worlds is genuine, and, as technologies develop, the possibilities for group mourning and rites expand.

On December 2, 2008, Jessica Curry and Dan Pinchbeck (or Trixiebelle Landar and Caspar Helendale in Second Life) invited users to join together in a virtual mausoleum in Second Life to mourn the loss of deleted avatars in a performance called *The Second Death of Caspar Helendale*:

> They constructed a monument to these lost avatars, where the audience was able to join them for a virtual vigil. This included a specially composed requiem for the departed; and a Book of the Dead, containing the names of the lost and their reasons for leaving their second lives. At the end of the performance, Caspar joined the ranks of abandoned avatars and relinquished his second life. (2ndlive.org, 2009)

What Curry and Pinchbeck draw attention to with this project is the death of the *identity* represented by the avatar, rather than the mortal body of the user. Whether or not the mourning process of the users was comparable to a real-world funerary ritual, or merely novelty, was based on individual experiences. Either way, as the deaths of avatars in on-line realities continue to affect the lives of those in the real world, artists must be there to put both their physical and simulated bodies in the fray, both on and off the screen, to show that the concept of "deletion" is more than just the press of a button.

References

2ndlive.org. 2009. http://www.2ndlive.org/projects/ps4.php (accessed on September 15, 2009)

Athey, Ron April 5, 2008. Conversation with the author.

Baudrillard, J., Poster, Mark ed. 1988. *Selected Writings* Davis: Stanford University Press.

Bauman, Z. 2003. *Liquid Love* Cambridge: Polity Press.

Daly, Matt. 2008. "Blending Realities. . .Done With Redundancy. . .on collective immersion through blended reality performance" Author's personal website. http://www.boogaloogames.net/bliargh/juegos/redundancy/redundancy designdoc.html (accessed on 11/17/2008)

Keidan, Lois and Morgan, Stuart eds. 1988 *Franko B* London: Black Dog Press.

Mattes, Eva and Franco. 2008. "Nothing is Real, Everything is Possible" excerpts from interviews on artists' personal site. http://www.0100101110101101.org/home/performances/interview.html (accessed on 11/18/2008)

Montano, L. 2000. *performance artists talking in the eighties* Berkeley: University of California Press.

Satter, Raphael. 2008 "Virtual Affair Leads to Real Divorce for UK Couple" *Associated Press* November 14, 2008 http://news.yahoo.com/s/ap/20081114/ap_on_re_eu/eu_britain_virtual_affair;_ylt=AlkHFa0wpWu1dMfI6NieVQ90bBAF (accessed 11/17/1008)

Stitt, A. 2001 *Small Time Life* London: Black Dog Press.

University of Guelph. 2009. "Facebook Causes Jealousy, Hampers Romance, Study Finds" News release. http://www.uoguelph.ca/news/2009/02/post_176.html (accessed on 02/12/2009)

Watkins, Thomas. 2008. "Jury convicts mom of lesser charges in online hoax" *Associated Press* November 26, 2008 http://news.yahoo.com/s/ap/20081126/ap_on_re_us/internet_suicide;_ylt=AiPRex3FRatQLfLA48XZC4ZvzwcF (accessed on 11/26/2008)

Wolff, Rachel. 2008. "All the Web's a Stage" *ARTnews* Vol. 107, Number 2. February 2008 http://www.artnewsonline.com/issues/article.asp?art_id=2443 (accessed 11/16/2008)

Yamaguchi, Mari. 2008."Online Divorcee Jailed After Killing Virtual Hubby" *Associated Press* October 23, 2008. http://news.yahoo.com/s/ap/20081023/ap_on_re_as/as_japan_avatar_murder (accessed on 10/23/08)

CHAPTER SEVEN

PERFORMING IN THE ACOUSTIC ARENA: THE ROLE OF THE PORTABLE AUDIO DEVICE IN A USER'S EXPERIENCE OF URBAN PLACE

RACHEL O'DWYER

Introduction

> "For twenty-five centuries, western knowledge has tried to look upon the world. It has failed to understand that the world is not for beholding. It is for hearing. It is not legible, but audible."[1]
> —Jacques Attali

> "The Sony Walkman has done more to change human perception than any virtual reality gadget. I can't remember any technological experience since that was quite so wonderful as being able to take music and move it through landscapes and architecture."[2]
> —William Gibson

A common phenomenon now shapes everyday urban experience: moving through the city to music. The predominant listening practice of the twenty first century city dweller is channelled in this fashion, fed through earbuds, and presented against the backdrop of an urban stage; the streets thronged with pedestrians, on public transport and passing through urban arenas, all moving, all listening. This is an auditory experience that involves a contextualisation of urban space and human mobility. It describes a culture in which our mobile devices are increasingly ubiquitous; where private soundscapes and public urban spaces intersect. How is this auditory phenomenon shaping the urban experience of the user?

This paper explores how the use of portable audio devices, such as the mp3 player or walkman, plays a role in generating a user's experience of urban place. It focuses not only on the role of sound and mobility in urban spatial practices, but on how actors and environments converge to produce notions of place in the contemporary city. Urban studies and media technologies intersect in the following analysis. Where our mobile and ambient devices increasingly contribute to the everyday constitution of the urban fabric, mediating and managing our experience of that environment, it will be argued that the use of a portable audio device is a mobile listening experience that not only *takes* place within the city, it *makes* place: the everyday act of moving and listening to sound is a performative activity that shapes urban experience and constitutes place.

This paper arises out of recently identified problems concerning the quality of contemporary urban experience. Criticisms centre on an increased atomisation in everyday life, on the loss of public and social spaces in the city to commercial and privatised institutions, and on the progressive regulation of individual agencies in the urban environment. Where understandings of place prefigure forms of sociability, relativity and local identity, critics now argue that 'place' and 'the city' are mutually exclusive terms. Instead we increasingly inhabit what anthropologist Marc Augé terms "non-places",[3] indicating spaces which are not anthropologically produced so much as defined by transmission, networked movements and the flow of objects and information through their boundaries. More and more, today's urban environments are figured as coded spaces of automated management, where inhabitants commune with absent others or retreat into private dialogues with artefacts of the culture industry, where mediated spaces manifest to reduce sociability and keep inhabitants focused on "action as opposed to interaction".[4] In this vein, the portable audio device is pejoratively defined as absenting the user from an 'immediate' urban experience, and forms of co-present interaction.

Contrary to this perspective, the following discussion focuses on the role the user plays in shaping mobile devices towards meaningful and shared experiences of urban place. If the quality of urban experience is said to be decreasing, if 'places', as conduits for meaningful, social, and public interaction, are said to be disappearing from the city, it is necessary to identify ways of potentially enriching our environment. Where physical infrastructures, technological artefacts and human actors intersect in the contemporary city, how might our media devices contribute to, rather than absent, the user from urban place? What role does the user of a portable audio device play in generating geo-spatial content?

To structure this discussion, the argument is divided into three sections. The first section maintains that how we understand and engage with place is transformed by moving to sound, and suggests that a revised concept of place that affords sound and mobility is a powerful tool for better understanding the everyday use of portable audio devices. This leads to a discussion in the second section, which details the role of the portable audio device in the management of urban experience, as a technology that facilitates the interconnection of physical and virtual contexts within the city. The third section reframes an understanding of the relationship between users, devices, and environmental contexts, proposing ways in which the auditory space of the mobile device could be augmented to produce networked and socially cohesive experiences of place that progress beyond the individuated sonic experience of a mobile listener.

Reconsidering Place through Sound and Movement

In theorising the relationship between mobile media and place, a key issue is that while place is increasingly recognised as important in critical literature, how this concept is conventionally applied is inadequate for understanding the role played by portable audio devices in an urban context. This arguably requires a reconsideration of traditional understandings of place to emphasise the role of multimodal qualities such as sound and movement in its production. Furthermore, in a mediatised environment, it requires a consideration of the relationship between users and mobile devices where both are agents in the performance of place.

The author's use of the term 'place', therefore, understands it to be a condition that progresses beyond the static geographical conduit towards a relational ontology contingent on human action, technological mediation, and the forms of social relations that occur therein. Place is subject to the interactions that produce it as relational, historical and concerned with identity. This definition of place situates itself in relation to a broader discourse concerning pervasive computing and urban development, exploring the potential of information technology and networked infrastructures to positively influence urban spaces. Where portable audio devices form a large part of everyday urban practice, this is a user-device relationship that continually shapes urban experience and requires our consideration.

It might be suggested that alternative sensory modalities provide new forms of agency for the inhabitants of the urban environment, representing sensorial strategies for opening non-places back up to forms of identity, relationality and interaction. It is necessary to consider place apart from visual epistemologies and locate practices foreign to the traditionally panoptic or theoretical constructions that abound, moving instead towards what Michel de Certeau refers to as an "opaque and blind mobility",[5] a way of being in place that is not pre-occupied with visual experience.

The writings of theorists such as de Certeau and Henri Lefebvre are frequently cited by those who wish to reconstitute 'place' to include human mobility, understanding walking as an inherently tactical activity that establishes an intimate form of contact with place. Pedestrian mobility, for De Certeau, is understood as a spatial 'acting-out' of place, and implies relations among differentiated positions, among territories and among individuals.[6] More recently, disciplines such as human geography and embodied cognition have emphasised the role of ambulatory, tactile and peripatetic practices in shaping conceptual metaphors and rational thought. This suggests a revised concept of place that understands it as produced not so much by physical infrastructures and topographies as through practical mechanisms such as walking at the level of the street.

If being in place involves a whole set of physical performances that are constantly evolving as people traverse their environment, it is necessary to address how this reconfigures our understanding of the role of mobile devices in the urban arena. If walking is fundamental to human engagement with place, then the use of mobile media represents a significant impact on this experience. Through connecting with others or producing virtual soundscapes whilst moving through the city, the user contributes to the social construction of the urban environment. As performances that are frequently nested in the context of urban mobility, their use becomes a part of the everyday rhythms of the city which usher that place into being and invest it with meaning.

If movement itself is a constructive activity, then moving to sound is even more so. Acoustics have always functioned to create places and underline the conditions that go hand in hand with its production: boundaries, soundmarks and notions of civic space, as well as fostering the forms of relational behaviour that make up a place. Many theorists who currently examine the relationship between urban space and sound would suggest that the use of sonic technology provides an oblique entry into these visually regulated spaces. Several academic studies have recently examined the role of sonic media in broadcasting cultural identities in place. In these instances, noise, as was recognised by Jacques Attali, affords the possibility to reconfigure the qualities of a concrete space.[7] Sociologist Sebastian Ureta, who has explored the use of sound in low-incoming housing estates, maintains that many individuals today feel powerless in relation to the possibilities for control and transformation of their material space. They instead use alternative means to manage and appropriate their environments. One such strategy is the use of sound, which becomes a way of wresting control of a space.[8] A further example of this is detailed in Julian Henriques' account of what he terms 'sonic dominance', describing a situation in which sound, and in particular excessive and physically disruptive levels, is produced as the dominant sensory modality and used to foreground local identities. For Henriques, sonic dominance facilitates a specific sense of *place*, rather than a general abstract idea of space.

> "It is unique, immediate, and the place of tradition and ritual performance...sonic space [is] the antithesis to the non-places of airports, shopping malls, high streets and ATM aprons that Marc Augé discusses. Sonic spaces are fully impregnated with the living tradition of the moment."[9]

Sound becomes a way to negotiate the non-places of the urban environment. Where visual epistemologies of place are frequently so over-determined by the logic of late capitalism – to the extent that it is difficult to speak of such spaces in terms of agency or performance, sound, as a form of spatial organisation that is frequently overlooked, provides an arena in which normative codes do not fix, or are perhaps fixed differently. Where both sound and movement play a vital role in constructing urban experience, this has consequences for how we conceive of portable audio devices. The device in this context, rather than absenting the user from place, provides agency precisely in its ability to manage and reconstitute civic space into meaningful place. Place is generated by the mobile experience of the user.

Hybrid Places: The Acoustic Arena of the Portable Audio Device

The use of the portable audio device largely functions to produce *privatised* soundscapes within the urban environment. The user's experience is highly individuated, and largely confined to the binaural conduit of the listening device. It has been argued that as geographical notions of personal space become harder to substantiate, the construction of a mediated and privatised conceptual space becomes a common strategy for urban citizens[10]. The personal space of the listener is figured as a virtual or conceptual space, affording the user the possibility to overlay the concrete city with a virtual acoustic arena. It follows that sonic technologies in many ways produced the possibility for virtual places before these were realised within the architectonics of cyberspace.

There is currently an oblique suggestion that the failings of physical urban planning to produce public place can be addressed within the architecture of cyberspace. The greater agency afforded by virtual environments, compared to the restricted social codes of the urban arena, suggest that the space for future social interaction will be technologically enabled. For many theorists, "being able to occupy a virtual space implies that one can have the benefits of physicality without being bound by its limitations",[11] moving beyond the confines of geographical distances and the repressive habits inherited by industrial society. This utopian view of cyberspace has been contested on the grounds of an idealistic coupling of cyber architecture and notions of social democracy, but furthermore on its disregard for the role of sensorial and embodied productions of place, privileging the visuo-centric epistemologies of virtual reality in the construction of experience over everyday spatial practices. As technologies which are fundamentally concerned with our negotiation and engagement with place and space, mobile media render such escapist visions less attractive, and arguably less tenable.

Rather, the ubiquity of mobile media in urban space has led to what is termed the 'hybridisation of space' understood as multiple modes of place existing in conjunction within a physical conduit. Portable audio devices are arguably the first instance in which this form of spatial enfolding takes place, blending the physical spaces moved through with the virtual soundscape the user carries with her.

However, it is necessary to identify the points of connection occurring between this acoustic space and the concrete spaces traversed. These spaces, as Michael Bull argues, are habitually limited in their forms of co-present interaction: the experience of moving to sound that the mp3 player facilitates is largely individuated.[12] Where the device has the technicity to produce meaningful places for the city dweller, these binaural conduits are representative of Zygmunt Bauman's urban citizens who "whatever company they wish to keep, they carry with them, like snails carry their homes".[13] Recalling the understanding of place as contingent in part on relational behaviours, it is necessary to question how these personal experiences might be augmented or *networked* to produce a collective experience necessary to the production of place. The following explores some of the ways in which users are re-shaping portable audio devices towards sociable practice and shared spatial experience.

User-Generated Place: The Social Construction of Mobile Music

The history of mobile media demonstrates that portable music consumption was socially shaped towards a solitary listening practice equated with the reification of the sound 'object'. Where the predominant use of portable audio devices is socially atomised, it is necessary to identify strategies which suggest alternative user-device relationships in urban place. This approach draws on theories from the Social Construction of Technology (SCOT), a branch of science and technology studies which explores how artefacts are socially shaped, through various stages of ideation and flexibility, and through the influence of relevant social groups.[14] While any broad overview of the SCOT methodology is beyond the scope of this paper, it will briefly address the theories of 'interpretative flexibility' and 'closure' which describe the passage of an artefact from plastic and flexible interpretations through to a habitual and closed practice of use. This states that when a technology is initially introduced there are myriad interpretations for how it might be understood and used which gradually give way to a more universal and fixed user-device relationship. However, it can be demonstrated that the habitual user-device relationships that convene around an artefact are not immutable practices – but what Madeleine Akrich would term 'scripts' embodying variable degrees of flexibility. [15] The possibility always exists to 'de-script' a technology; to open it back up to alternative performances.

It can be argued that 'interpretative flexibility' is particularly relevant to sonic technologies. Technologies which record, transmit and disseminate sound within the urban arena are open to flexible forms of use. Often the only factors which distinguish these as discrete media forms are the ways in which they are habitually used. In the history of sonic media, according to Jonathan Sterne, connections between function, practice, institution and network – call them point-to-point, broadcast, archival – were not clearly assigned to a single technology over another.[16]

The task, therefore, is to locate alternative scripts in mobile media consumption that encode new forms of sociability in the urban environment. It follows that an examination of relatively new forms of mobile media, such as the mp3 player or iPhone, may possess a higher degree of interpretative flexibility, as they have yet to stabilise and achieve closure.

An example of this is the social phenomenon of on-line file sharing, emerging from mp3 formatting. Compression techniques designed to allow a large quantity of music to be stored on a portable device had an incidental effect on modes of consumption and distribution, where these files are suitable for live streaming and download via the internet. This in turn facilitates the development of forms of on-line social networking involving the distribution of mp3 file formats through websites such as Limewire, BitTorrent and PirateBay.[17] These witness relational practices of music consumption in the public virtual domain, frequently occurring alongside practices such as on-line group discussion, public forums, message boards and FTP posts.

Another practice known as 'jack-sharing' has been documented in different parts of the United States and the United Kingdom. This involves a physical interaction between two mp3 players and users in a public space, where listeners on public transport or passing in the street connect their audio jack to a stranger's portable device and listen to music. It may be suggested that 'jack-sharing' is a legacy of on-line file sharing, comprising a lo-fidelity version of what some predict to be the future application of mobile media, whereby the network migrates from the traditional desktop model towards a pervasive broadcasting utility supported by Bluetooth or adhoc networking capabilities.

Similarly, as mobile devices become increasingly amorphous, often combining mobile communicative and wifi capabilities with the capacity for entertainment, they afford new ways of conceiving mobile media in terms of ludic practices in mobile communications use. The ubiquity of mobile communication devices and the ways in which they, like the portable audio device, have come to signify a performance or extension of the self in the public and virtual arena, are facilitating the merging of playful and social behaviours with the everyday urban environment. For example, and contra Marc Augé, it has been argued that mobile phone users have created a new use for urban and transitional spaces, transforming non-place into a ludic sphere for social interactions. Mobile media becomes a way to renegotiate rather than circumvent physical urban places. If we consider the current design strategies surrounding mp3 players as they progress towards a ubiquitous networking device, the forms of interaction convening around virtual platforms and wireless devices could be re-scripted for portable audio device use.

Conclusion

The technologies for portable music consumption do not entail a specific predetermination that permits them, as Latour has put it, to pass through a neutral social medium.[18] Rather, the social medium the technology is embedded in – listeners moving through the city – will shape and be shaped by that technology. Of significance, therefore, are the practices of production and consumption which develop around the artefact. These practices, over time, may produce relationships between a user and a device which crystallise particular social, civil, or environmental behaviours whilst discouraging others. Pertinent in these examples is the role the user of a technology plays in shaping the mobile device. The shift towards the ludic, the social, and the interactive within mobile listening experience are the products of the *user*'s intervention in the script for that technology. This suggests a necessity to look outside traditional design imperatives to the role of user-generated-content in shaping the mobile device and, consequently, the urban context in which it is used.

The argument presented here is positioned in opposition to a critical approach which describes the use of portable audio devices as a strategy for absenting the user from place. This paper has instead explored the use of portable audio devices as a potential place-making activity, arguing that moving through sound provides utility to actively transform and shape the environment, through sensorial experience, through the construction of acoustic arenas, and through the potential networking of personal experience to produce a socially cohesive representation of urban place. Where critical discourses figure the mobile listener as a passive consumer in dialogue with the culture industry, the everyday use of the device to reconfigure and manage the coordinates of the built environment suggests that the role of the user progresses beyond consumption, to become an active producer of place. This poses questions with regard to the future implementation of strategies for urban development in the informational society, implying a re-shaping of the device to facilitate public broadcast and performance through the channels of current research into pervasive computing. Where the subject of this paper positions itself in relation to questions of user-generated-content in virtual platforms, the use of the portable audio device progresses beyond the dichotomy of embodied and virtual experiences, towards a performance that is nested within the corporeal, multimodal and informational contexts of the everyday city. Furthermore, as current trends in urban planning suggest a shift towards pervasive computing as a strategy for urban development, the hybrid space of the portable audio device suggests the possibility to shape and reconfigure that environment through sound, movement, and forms of sonic networking.

Notes

[1] Jacques Attali. *Noise: The Political Economy of Music* (Manchester: Manchester University Press, 1985)

[2] William Gibson. *Interview: Time Out* (6 October 1993)

[3] Marc Augé. *Non-Places: Introduction to an Anthropology of Supermodernity* (London: Verso, 1995)

[4] Zygmunt Bauman. *Liquid Modernity* (Cambridge: Polity Press, 2002)

[5] Michel de Certeau. *The Practice of Everyday Life* (London: California University Press, 1984)

[6] ibid.

[7]Attali, op.cit

[8] Sebastian Ureta. "Noise and the Battles for Space: Mediated Noise and Everyday life in a Social Housing Estate in Santiago, Chile" *New Media and Society* (2007): 103-130

[9] Julian Henriques. *Sonic Dominance and the Reggae Sound System Session* (London: Berg, 2003)

[10] Michael Bull. *Sound Moves: Ipod Culture and Urban Experience* (London: Routledge, 2007)

[11] Katherine Hayles cited in Allesandro Aurigi. *Making the Digital City* (London, Ashgate, 2005)

[12] Bull. op.cit

[13] Bauman. op.cit

[14] Pinch, Trevor J. and Wiebe E. Bijker. The Social Construction of Facts and Artefacts: Or How the Sociology of Science and the Sociology of Technology Might Benefit Each Other. Social Studies of Science 14 (August 1984): 399-441.

[15] Madeleine Akrich. *The Description of Technological Objects* (London: MIT Press, 1997)

[16] Jonathan Sterne. *The Audible Past* (London: Duke University Press, 2003)

[17] http://www.limewire.com, http://www.bittorrent.com, http://www.piratebay.com

[18] Bruno Latour. *Science in Action* (United States of America: Harvard University Press, 1987)

CHAPTER EIGHT

AROUND THE WORLD IN FIVE SECONDS: CHALLENGES AND OPPORTUNITIES IN DESIGNING SONIC TRAVEL

ALAIN B. RENAUD

Introduction

The field of network music performance is a growing discipline and an important example of demonstrating the use of advanced technologies in performance. Applying the idea of fast sonic travel over geographically displaced spaces is an application of network music performance that has the most potential. This allows the development of performative strategies and technologies that use the network and remote spaces as the core for interactions. In parallel, user-generated content portals are flourishing all over the Internet through blogs, wikis and social networks such as Facebook or Twitter as well as user-centric sharing sites such as YouTube. By definition, user-generated content is the creation of information or material that is created by users themselves (Beck 2007). It is also very much associated with Web 2.0, a new generation of the Internet where network content is built by users rather than providers and aggregators. In terms of software programming or code generation Web 2.0 strategies are focusing on building *collective intelligence* algorithms (Segaran 2007), allowing not only content but also applications to be built by Internet users. Network music performance and sonic travel are very much part of this evolution by placing collective knowledge and practice as the central elements for generating content that is disparate, displaced and fragmented across multiple network nodes. An essential aspect to allow users to participate in the distributed content creation process is to devise strategies for sonic travel that take the network as well as multiple sites and users as a core element of the content creation process.

Disparate content creation

The last ten years have seen the birth of many initiatives ranging from the development of software applications and strategies to allow *"better than real"* low delay high-quality communication across long distances (Chafe, Wilson et al. 2000). It has led to comprehensive frameworks and initiatives such as Disparate Bodies (Rebelo, 2009), a series of collaborative events that use the network as a core for interconnecting performers and audiences across multiple sites or the Net.Vs.Net collective, a group that only conceptualizes, composes and performs over very long distances. Through initiatives such as the ones cited above, geographically displaced content creators and performers over several physical locations are becoming realistic and the creation of user-generated content in a fragmented manner is emerging naturally from the individual contributions of the peers connected to the network. In this context, user-generated content becomes the result of distributed authorship. According to Roy Ascott, the *"distance makes the art grow further"* (Chandler, Neumark 2005). Indeed, distributed minds create content that is the result of assembling, connecting and meshing knowledge into one piece of art. Therefore, this artwork would become disjunct and meaningless if the network interconnecting those minds was removed.

Depending on the set-up, the network will play an important role in providing or adding its own acoustical features that can be used as part of the distributed content creation and the resulting performance. An additional factor to consider is the interconnection of several physical acoustic spaces over the network and how they contribute in shaping network music performance environments. Depending on the approach, the combination of disparate acoustic environments can lead to either a large networked space or a combination of spaces in which sound can travel across, meet and morph. This has the potential to create an ever-changing acoustic environment in which sound can travel and be influenced by the specific environment in which it is located. This approach paves the way for the realisation of network centric acoustic environments in which sound can be injected, moved around and transformed thus becoming an integral part of the composition or/and performance process. I call this series of approaches *Sonic Travel* with sound elements such as performers or simple sound objects such as oscillators that are traveling across physical spaces, such as rooms and concert halls and virtual spaces such as the network distance between nodes or the injection of such objects in virtual environments. The combination of elements mentioned above provide the users with a palette of tools and sound objects that allow them to shape network-centric compositions that are the results of their input and their interactions with local and remote environments and users.

A first implementation of some of the elements mentioned here and later in the text was conducted during a recent Net Vs. Net Collective concert during which I premiered *Crossovers*[1], a structured improvisation for two dislocated performers between the Center for Computer Research in Music and Acoustics (CCRMA) in Stanford and the Sonic Arts Research Centre (SARC) in Belfast. A graphic score indicated the location of the performers in each space and allowed them to interact based on their physical location within the distributed virtual and physical spaces. The presence of the network and the two acoustically distinct spaces captured as ambisonic streams enhanced the sonic space in which the performers interacted.

Figure 1: Snapshot of Crossovers score

Acoustics revisited

The combination of the *Network Distance* (the physical distance between two network nodes) combined with interconnected physical spaces form an acoustic environment with its own particularities such as multiple early reflections and reverberations. It is therefore worth providing a basic background of acoustic theories to better understand the functioning of acoustics and how it relates to a networked situation and how the network has the potential to behave as an acoustic medium in itself.

Using the network as a virtual acoustic space was first initiated by network music pioneers like Atau Tanaka and Kasper Toeplitz who designed an art installation, Global String, which interconnected two arts galleries. The installation is described on the Global String website as a, "*multi-site network music installation, connected via the Internet. It is a musical instrument where the network is the resonating body of the instrument, by use of a real time sound synthesis server*" (Tanaka 2004). The principle behind Global String is to use the network as an extension of the physical strings on both sites and use the network as a resonating apparatus. A real string is attached to the floor on one end and to a wall on the other end. Sensors then capture the vibrations of the string and convert the vibration into a physical model, which is conveyed by the network.

Another approach to network acoustics is the one developed by Chris Chafe in a paper called *Levels of Temporal Resolution in Sonification of Network Performance* (Chafe, Leistikow 2001). The paper introduces the concept of sonification of ping commands, a series of small network packets sent from one node to another, to evaluate the quality of services (QoS) of networks. The concept was further implemented in the Ping installation in San Francisco, which allowed users to hear ping commands to many nodes around the world (Chafe 2007).

In the examples above, interconnection between network nodes uses the analogy of a simple string. There can be one string linking two nodes and a second string if three nodes are involved and so on. Choosing to represent networks acoustically as a succession of strings gives a good graphical impression of a network connection linking spaces. Several network parameters can be applied to the string, which in acoustic terms will translate into a change of length or stiffness. Strings that are in a vibrating state take the form of standing waves and will produce a fundamental frequency in the first mode. The mode of vibration will also depend on tension, the mass and the length of the string. Moreover, depending on the mode of excitation of the string a particular mix of harmonics will be produced. For example, if a string is plucked or bowed, the set of harmonics produced will be different and the timbre will vary considerably. The distance between network nodes is also important in determining the way we can use the strings spanning around a network. Depending on the distance between nodes, particular pitches and sonic artifacts are generated. When we consider the network as an acoustic entity in itself, it is important to look at how sound behaves when it travels through air. Sound travels at a speed of roughly 340 meters per second if certain conditions are met such as optimum constant temperature, optimal humidity and the lack of interferences (Cutnell, Johnson 2007). If a sound source (A) is away from a listener (B), it will take a certain amount of time for (A) to get to (B). The distance is the factor that separates (A) from (B) and logically, the longer the distance the longer the time gap will be between (A) and (B) as shown in [Figure 2].

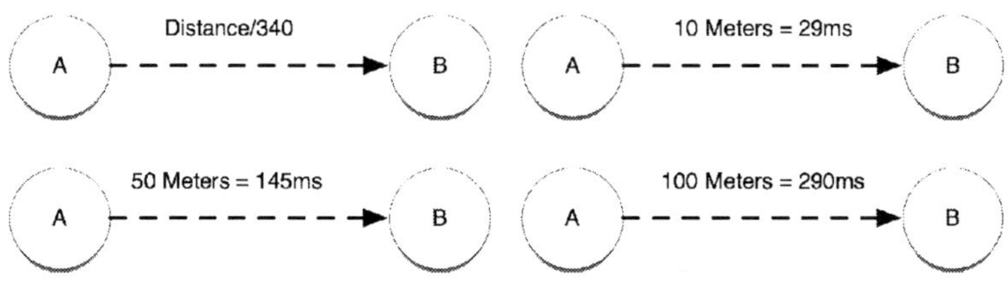

Figure 2: Speed of sound and distance

This example would work in a perfectly neutral acoustic environment such as an anechoic chamber. In a neutral anechoic environment, almost none of the frequencies are reflected back thanks to specially engineered surfaces, which are able to absorb any potential reflections. The main quality brought by an anechoic chamber is the lack of echoes in which a typical anechoic chamber will absorb 99.9% of incident sound waves (Blesser, Salter 2007). This provides an acoustically "dead" environment, virtually free of reflections, and as a result, is extremely quiet. However, in most acoustic spaces, the sound source will encounter a number of obstacles. This phenomenon will not only delay the delivery of the sound source to the listener but will also create secondary reflections in the sound path, leading to the delivery of de-multiplied sound sources that reach the listener (B) with time-shifted versions of the original sound source.

Depending on the type and length of the reflections, the delayed delivery of the sound source will lead to either an echo like effect, reverberation or both.

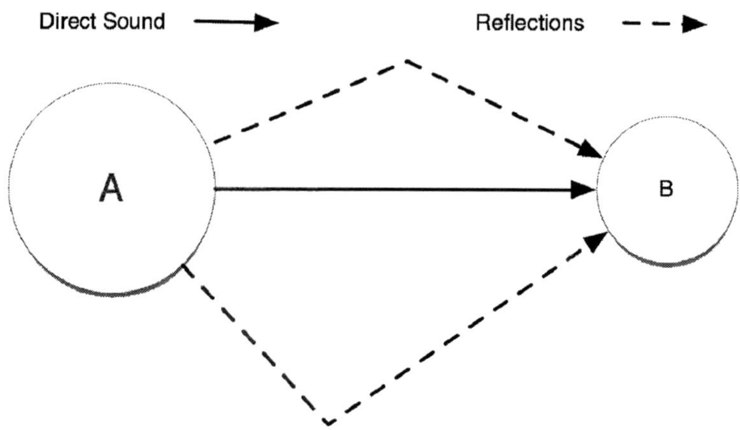

Figure 3: Direct sound and reflections

When taking the concept of sound traveling through a medium such as air to a network configuration, the speed of sound becomes, conceptually, the speed of light as the data packets sent from (A) to (B) travel through fiber optics networks, at least at the backbone level. Therefore, the distances between two network nodes can be translated acoustically in milliseconds from the sound source (A) to the listener (B). However, it is important to mention that the data on current network infrastructure does not travel at the speed of light. The speed of light in a vacuum is 299,792,458 meters per second (Lehrman 1998); therefore network traffic is not able to achieve such speed because of the various switches it needs to go through and the potential degradation of the traffic by various network conditions leading to lost packets. In addition, the conversion of audio signals from analogue to digital need to be taken into account when calculating the time it takes for the sound source (A) to reach the listener (B). In addition, the path that a signal takes over a network is potentially quite complex as it will not travel from one point to another, *"as the crow flies,"* by taking the shortest route between two points. Instead, the signal will take the path determined by the network topology between two nodes. For this purpose, I call the distance between two networked nodes, the *Network Distance.*

Translating the Network Distance into acoustics

If we return to the principles of acoustics outlined earlier in the chapter, we can take again the analogy of a string spanning from one node to another, which are used as oscillators. If we start from a central point called Control Node and reach various Distant Nodes simultaneously (such as A, B, C, D, E and F), we will fill synthesis elements (such as a sine wave) to six different Network Distances, which are not equidistant. As a result, we will get six different frequencies back to the Control Node. This is equivalent to six direct sound paths that are bounced from a sound source (Control Node) to a listener (Distant Node) and fed back to the listener.

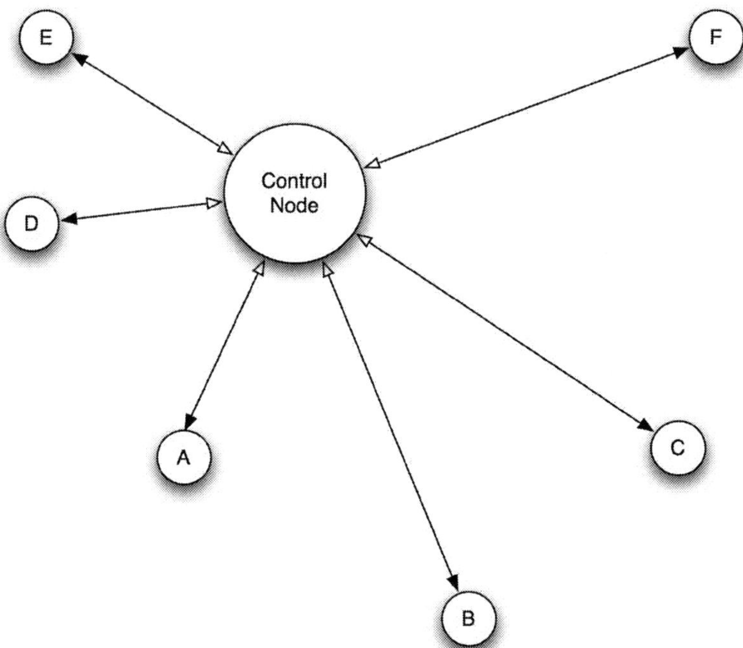

Figure 4: Control and Distant Nodes, basic topology

In this basic case, the relationship between the Control Node and the Distant Node is straightforward and sonically not very rewarding. If we add the possibility to control the amount of delay that we set from the Control Node to the Distant Nodes and include the ability to calculate the interdependencies between the nodes, the principle becomes more meaningful. It is important, of course, to understand that there will always be an original delay value, which cannot be decreased but only increased. However, this initial value is useful to us, as it acts as the fundamental frequency in acoustic terms. So, if we go back to the basic topology and start artificially stretching the distance from the Control Node to the Distant Nodes, the respective frequencies will change. In this case, we will use the distance between the Control Node and the Distant Node F as the fundamental as it is the longest Network Distance of all nodes. All the other relationships will be harmonics of the fundamental. In [Figure **4**], the harmonic relationship between the Control Node and the Distant Nodes are non-existent. However, we can render the Network Distance in a more meaningful way by artificially adding distance (delay in this case) to the various Distant Nodes so that they achieve a mathematical relationship related to the fundamental, in this case the distance between the Control Node and the Distant Node F. The resulting relationship will be as follows if we build a harmonic scenario based on Distant Node F as being the fundamental:

> Control Node to Distant Node F = 1f (the fundamental)
> Control Node to Distant Node 2 = 2f (twice the frequency of the fundamental, hence the shorter Network Distance)

This principle can also be applied to the other Distant Nodes based on the fundamental (1f). The resulting effect is a polyphonic synthesizer that uses the network as a succession of oscillators. Adding acoustic reflections of the waveforms generated by the Control Node can increase the complexity of the system even more. In the case of network acoustics, we can artificially bounce the waveforms from one Distant Node to another and send them back though the reflected node. [Figure 5] illustrates one of the possible configurations. In this case, the Control Node sends a signal to Distant Node F.

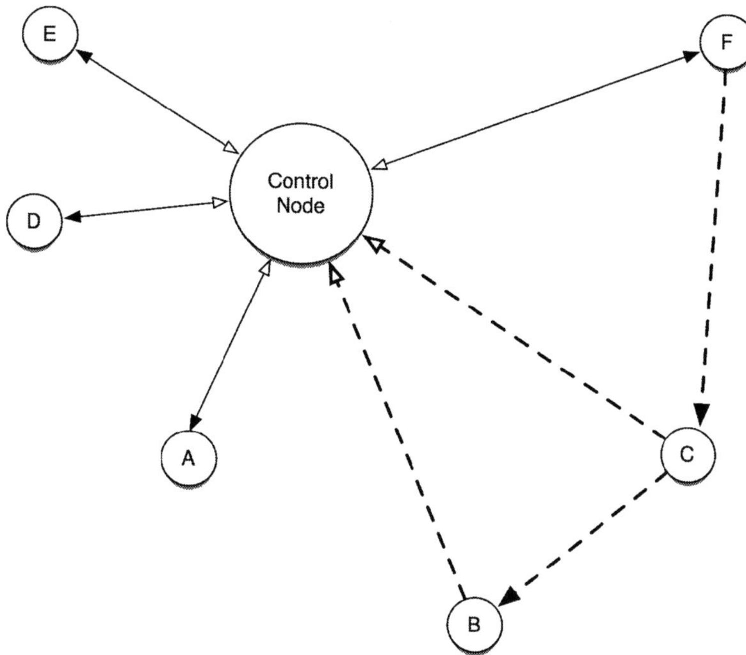

Figure 5: Reflected nodes

F still feeds back to the Control Node but also bounces the signal directly to C, which in turns then sends it back to the Control Node. C also sends the signal directly to B and the signal is sent back to the Control Node as well via B. This complex interlocking creates reflections that are being created by the Network Distance. Many other configurations, which are assignable by the Control Node, are possible. The latter process can be seen as an analogy to patching analogue synthesizers except that in this case, the Control Node is used as a central patch with attributes or modules scattered all over the network.

This series of examples demonstrates that based on the initial ideas of Chafe and Tanaka, the network can be used as a complex instrument, which is intrinsic to the network itself.

The concepts outlined so far are considering the connections between nodes as an ever changeable and shapeable succession of strings across a network. In order for the theory to be complete and to implement our scenarios, we need to also consider the addition of physical environments, such as rooms or concert halls that are interconnected by the arrangement of strings and how they contribute to the overall picture. It is indeed important to think about the consequences of opening the network to various distant real acoustic spaces. When we add acoustic spaces to the acoustic particulars generated by the network, we will need to adapt accordingly with additional reverberations, standing waves and echoes.

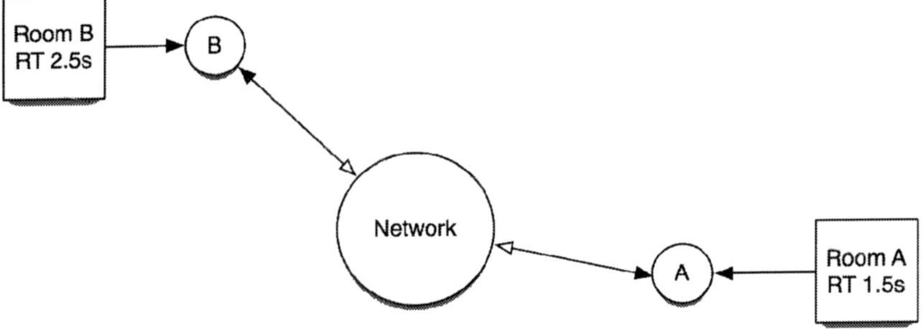

Figure 6: Acoustic and network combination

[Figure 6] demonstrates the combination of the network acoustic with the physical acoustics of two real spaces. In this case, Room A has a reverberation time of 1.5 seconds and Room B has a reverberation time of 2.5 seconds. If we perform over the network with acoustic instruments on both ends, the instrument in Room A will be embedded in the acoustics of Room A. The sound coming from Room B will have the acoustics of Room B combined with the acoustics of Room A as well as the acoustic features of the network itself. For Room B, it will be exactly the opposite. The potential offered by this arrangement can be meaningful and artistic but needs to be taken into account in the compositional process so that it does not become problematic. This arrangement borrows the acoustic particularities of distant spaces and expands the original space. However, one of the major issues to solve in this case is that even though the two instruments play together over the network, the perception of space and therefore, the perception of the performance itself will be different on each end.

The three approaches

The concepts outlined above have engendered a series of Sonic Travel scenarios in network music performance identified as Remote Acoustics, Eavesdropping and Sonic Partitioning. All scenarios are based on a three-node arrangement, providing a reasonable amount of complexity and flexibility.

When combining remote acoustic environments and Network Distances between them, the configuration will lead to an initial arrangement as illustrated below, which combines interconnected physical spaces (Node A, Node B and Node C), separated by network distances (L1 and L2).

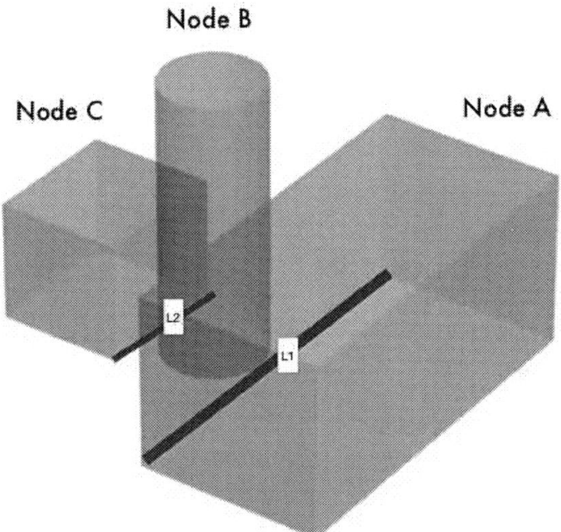

Figure 7: Initial physical spaces with Network Distances

By applying the initial arrangement to the first approach, Remote Acoustics, shown in [Figure **8**] we will start using the combined acoustic features of a local space in which two performers (P) are located and diffusing the sound of the performers in remote spaces. This arrangement allows the usage of live remote spaces and also, given that a multichannel configuration exists (at the capture and reproduction levels), a interpolation of sound from Node A to Node B and/or Node C as well as giving the sonic impression that sound revolves around or across the rooms.

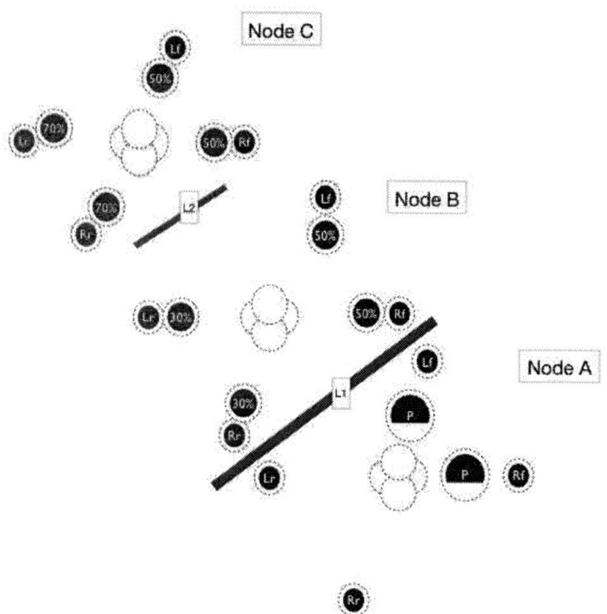

Figure 8: Remote Acoustics scenario

The second approach, Eavesdropping, shown in [Figure **9**] takes the same configuration of room arrangements as the one illustrated above but places the two performers (P) in two separate spaces. This configuration allows a typical network music performance to happen with two musicians interacting between Node A and Node B. In addition, Node C acts as a third environment, in which the two performers can virtually meet and interact into a remote physical space.

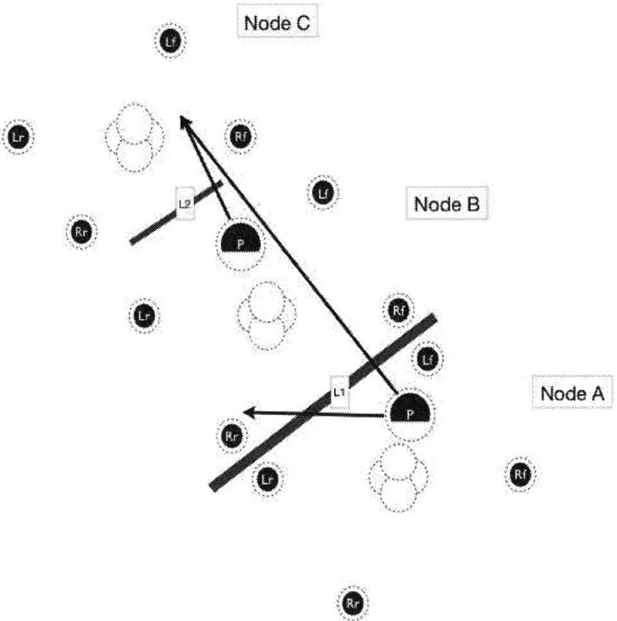

Figure 9: Eavesdropping scenario

The third and last scenario as shown in [Figure **10**] introduces the notion of Sonic Partitioning. In this scenario the acoustics of the physical spaces along with the network latencies between nodes are taken into account. The latency values between physical spaces can be controlled so that, for example, a performance would start with equal value latencies between the three nodes and then be changed through "delay fiddling", an action which allows the latency values to increase or decrease between nodes. In this case, the latency becomes part of the piece in itself. In the scenario below, there are three performers (P) on each node interacting initially across artificially evenly spaced spaces. As the piece progresses the latencies (L1 and L2) will vary, leading to the creation of delay patterns between spaces. Those network generated delay patterns will not be perceived identically depending on where the performers are located because of the different arrangement of latencies between nodes.

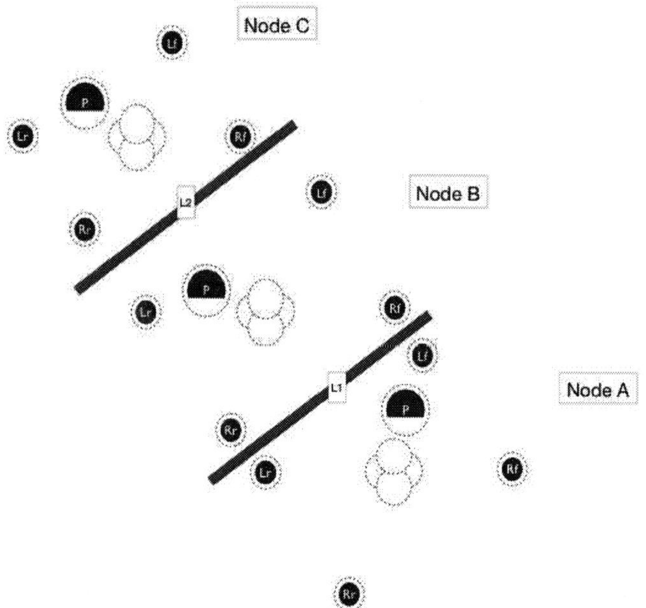

Figure 10: Sonic Partitioning scenario

Conclusion

Considering the combination of network acoustics and real acoustic environments with the latencies generated by the Network Distance between nodes provides a logical way to conduct network music performances across multiple spaces and uneven distances. It acts as a prime example of user-generated content across multiple sites and network conditions. The three scenarios outlined in this manuscript are the combination of research in network acoustics coupled with the concept that music can be composed and performed as a distributed initiative. Future work will include a more comprehensive implementation of the scenarios with the ultimate aim to provide a framework for distributed composition and performance, which could not happen without the network.

References

Beck, T., 2007. Web 2.0: User-Generated Content in Online Communities: A theoretical and empirical investigation of its Determinants. Diplomica Verlag.

Blesser, B. and Salter, L., 2007. Spaces speak, are you listening?: experiencing aural architecture. Cambridge, Mass.: MIT Press, c2007.

Caceres, J.-P., (2008), *Playing the network: the use of time delays as musical devices*. Proceedings of International Computer Music Conference (ICMC), Belfast, Northern Ireland, 2008.

Chafe, C. and Leistikow, R., 200. Levels of Temporal Resolution in Sonification of Network Performance. Proc. 2001 Intl. Conference on Auditory Display, Helsinki, 2001.

Chafe, C., Ping. 2007 http://ccrma-www.stanford.edu/~cc/pub/txthtml/ping.html Accessed 10 September 2009.

Chafe, C., Wilson, S., Leistikow, R., Chisholm, D. and Scavone, G., 2000. A Simplified Approach to High Quality Music and Sound Over IP. Proc. COSTG6 Conference on Digital Audio Effects (DAFx-00), Verona, 2000.

Chandler, A. and Neumark, N., 2005. At a distance: precursors to art and activism on the Internet. Cambridge, Mass.: MIT Press.

Cutnell, J.D. and Johnson, K.M., 2007. Physics. Hoboken, NJ : Wiley, c2007.

Lherman, R., 1998. Physics the easy way. New York Barron's [1998].

Rebelo, P. Disparate Bodies. 2009 http://www.sarc.qub.ac.uk/pages/db/ Accessed 29 August 2009.

Renaud, A, NetVsNet Collective. 2009 *http://www.netvsnet.com* Accessed 10 August 2009.

Segaran, T., 2007. Programming collective intelligence: building smart web 2. 0 applications. Sebastapol [CA] : O'Reilly.

Tanaka, A., Global String. 2004 http://www.sensorband.com/atau/globalstring/index2.html Accessed 10 September 2009.

Notes

[1] The piece was performed by Diana Siwiak at CCRMA and Justin Yang at SARC.

CHAPTER NINE

NETWORK[ED] LISTENING: EXPLORING A HAPTIC AURALITY

FRANZISKA SCHROEDER

This paper examines listening attitudes in network environments; in particular it considers networked music performances in which performers occupy disparate sites. The paper ties into the theme of user-generated content by looking at a specific network composition that relies on users to generate the compositional work. In this paper, I endeavour to shed light on the question of how the network itself makes us listen to ourselves, as well as to others. I take as a starting point Laura Marks' proposal for a haptic visuality (Marks, 2004) and suggest an analogous paradigm for listening; what I have come to entitle a *haptic aurality.* I argue that the network delineates particularly clearly the dialectic between two types of listening attitudes, which I will refer to as optical and haptic aural attitudes. The network, by means of its capacity to make distances sonically palpable, becomes an ideal platform for discussing intricacies in listening.

Touching with the eyes

In her paper from 2004 "*Haptic Visuality: Touching with the eyes*" Laura Marks argues for a haptic visuality as a type of seeing that uses the eye more like an organ of touch. In drawing parallels to listening, one can suggest a *haptic aurality* as a type of hearing that uses the ear like an organ of touch. The word haptic stems from the Greek "ἁφή – haphe", or ἁπτικός (*haptikos*), and pertains to the sense of touch; the Greek word "ἅπτεσθαι - haptesthai" meaning to "contact" or "touch" (Wikipedia).

I will consider notions of 'seeing' before investigating 'listening': we see different aspects of a non-sonic object by being close *and* by being able to separate ourselves from the object. In order to see and perceive an object, a picture or sculpture for instance, a move between 'optic' and 'haptic seeing', a distinction that Marks outlines, occurs. A visitor to a museum looking at a painting comes to mind. The seeing of the art-work is one of constant zooming in and out, whereby the 'see-er' approaches the picture and then distances himself from it. The 'see-er' wants to be close, literally needing to 'touch' the picture with his eyes. He engages in what Marks calls 'haptic looking' or 'haptic seeing', a type of gentle seeing that allows the eye to interact with, and indeed, to caress the surface of the object. During this type of seeing, according to Marks, we experience a loss of depth, not only in the object but also in ourselves; thus in haptic seeing we become susceptible to change, we become "amoebalike[1], lacking a center, changing as the surface to which we cling changes" (Marks, 2004). However, the 'see-er' also needs to stand back from the object; he needs to allow some distance between himself and the picture in order to mark out a more distinct and clearer relationship to the object. Marks refers to this as an 'optical visuality', a type of vision essential in that it allows the subject, the 'see-er', to delineate himself from the object. It allows the 'see-er' to see the object as distant and unconnected to himself. Marks argues that such a detached vision is useful when firing a missile for example; thus, the haptical space is an intimately lived-in space with tactile relations, where a close distance exists between oneself and the surroundings. Optical space, on the other hand, is divided; the 'see-er' needs to assume distance in order to map out the space, creating a clearly delineated territory.

Smooth and Striated

It is worth pointing out that Marks derives the notion of a haptic and optic visuality from the French philosophers Deleuze and Guattari (D&G) and their concepts of the 'smooth' and the 'striated'. In their seminal work "A Thousand Plateaus" (Deleuze and Guattari, 1988), they identify two types of space, a smooth and a striated space, or what they also refer to as nomad and sedentary space (ibid, p474). The city for instance is striated, whereas the sea is smooth. D&G also locate striated space in weaving, with its vertical and horizontal elements, in the elements' intertwining and perpendicular arrangements. Striated space is a space with a top and bottom. Embroidery for example represents striated space. Felt, however, constitutes smooth space, as there is no separation of threads; there are no fixed or mobile elements, distributing a continuous variation (ibid, p476). Smooth space is a nonformal space as found in patchwork.

In music D&G locate striated space in intertwined, fixed and variable elements. It is a space that organizes vertical (harmonies) and horizontal planes (melodies). Smooth space on the other hand is marked by continuous variation and development of form (ibid, p478). D&G argue that in striated space-time "one counts in order to occupy", whereas smooth space-time is occupied without counting (ibid, p477). Smooth is a 'nomos'[2], but striated always has a 'logos' (as the octave for example). Although it seems that there are clear delineations between these two spaces, between smooth and striated, or between haptic and optic space, it is essential to understand that Deleuze and Guattari also point to the combinatory possibilities of the two spaces. They argue that the two spaces exist only in mixtures, in the same way that Marks argues for the interdependency of optic and haptic vision. Deleuze and Guattari's interest lies in passages, in the combination of the two spaces. In recognising that there exist combinatory possibilities between the two spaces, D&G show us that this distinction is made in order to subordinate to this distinction the differences between 'haptic' and 'optic', 'close' and 'distant' vision (ibid, p496).

We can read this interdependency, or the combinatory possibilities of the haptic and optical seeing in parallel to the development of the sense of self in the newborn. In order to outline this argument I will digress slightly before returning to listening in the network. According to French psychoanalyst Jacques Lacan the development of the sense of self occurs in what he titles the "mirror stage". Lacan proposed that the human infant goes through a mirror stage, the primordial experience of identification, in which the infant identifies with an external image of the body, as seen in a mirror or as represented by his mother or carer. This image gives rise to the mental representation of an "I", an ideal image of him- or herself as an *imago*, an image, which is external to the infant. It gives rise to the infant's perception of "self" while at the same time establishes the ego as fundamentally dependent upon external objects. The foundation for all subsequent identifications is laid in this mirror stage: the "I" comes into being as the result of an encounter with an "other"[3]. This means that we attain an image of ourselves that allows us to establish relationships with other people and lets us negotiate the physical and social reality surrounding us.

One can argue that in newborns there exists a move from haptic to optic seeing: at first, the newborn is only able to see the face of his carer close up, and even then only blurred - the infant sees 'haptically' with a gentle distance between himself and the other. It is not surprising that the eye has not yet allowed the infant to distance itself, since the child needs the strong symbiotic relationship with his carer. The infant has not yet mastered a physical or emotional independence; the skins of both infant and carer become merged (in breast feeding for example) to allow for the child's dependency; thus, the infant feels and smells what the eye won't allow him to see. In due time, the newborn learns to "stand back". In the process of acquiring a more unified (though, as Lacan argues, ultimately unstable) sense of selfhood, and by being able to master a physical and emotional independence, the infant also learns to focus his eyes onto objects further away. By means of this further separation the child is able to see the other more clearly, and in being able to increase the distance between himself and the other, he learns to see more optically. This implies that the infant's experience of selfhood is bound up with the presence as well as with the dependence upon others and external objects. The infant develops a sense of "self" by means of separation.

It is worth noting that in this separation, in this movement from haptic to optic vision - so essential to the development of our sense of self - vision itself becomes a dominant sense. Other senses, such as smell and hearing for instance, are being pushed into the background. It is beyond the scope of this paper to tease out the argument about humans' apparent innate preference for vision over other senses. However, I would like to point to the writing of Don Ihde and his work "Listening and Voice: A Phenomenology of Sound", in which he develops this argument, stating that visualism has dominated our thinking about experience and human existence. Ihde criticises humans' common 'visual' way of thinking about the world – we tend to have a *worldview*. He uncovers a specific glory of vision that was already existent in Greek philosophical thought: the Greek language indeed aligns 'knowing' with 'seeing' and 'living' with 'beholding light' (Ihde, 1976, p7)[4]. In the mentioned work Ihde argues for a "deliberate decentering of visualism in order to point up the overlooked and the unheard", since, so Ihde contends, the praise of sight has led to an inattentiveness to the 'equal richness of listening' (ibid, p8). I therefore shall attend to the richness of 'listenings', exploring what I call network[ed] listening.

Network[ed] Listening

Whereas traditional performance spaces exude notions of unity, togetherness, coherence and situatedness (the concert hall for instance), the network's strengths are the opposite, being articulated by the superimposition of acoustics, the socially dynamic and the musically unknown. Elsewhere I have addressed strategies for dealing with the inherent properties of the network as performative environment (Schroeder et al, 2007). The network proposes the collision of multiple acoustic spaces, the inherent aural rendering of latency, and the displaced ensemble. One can argue that in a network environment there exist at least two types of listening spaces, a 'local' and a 'virtual' listening space. The two auditory spaces become particularly differentiated in networked music performances as performers perform in dispersed sites. As is often the case in these situations, the virtual space (as seen from space A, which I refer to as the 'local' space) tends to be a non-visual space, i.e. it is a space in a different physical location (space B), to which the performers in space A do not have the same visual access as the performers that occupy space B. In order to perform with musicians in different sites, it becomes a necessity that all performers have sonic access to all the spaces in a more or less reliable and equal fashion, although we know that these sonic representations of the individual spaces can never be exactly the same in all the sites[5]. This is not a new phenomenon since every listening situation delineates various different acoustic spaces: for instance, we listen to an orchestra 'locally', i.e. to the orchestra in the physical space itself as well as 'virtually', i.e. to the sonic reflections and re-fractions of the orchestral sound off the enclosed space. Although we know that the human ear is well equipped to bridge such sonic displacements if two simultaneous sounds are not displaced in time over 20ms [Hirsh, 1959], in a network music performance, the two types of listening spaces (local and virtual) are more clearly delineated than in the orchestral example. This is only partly due to the inherent physical distances and thus the differing acoustic properties of each space. More importantly and perhaps more interestingly, this delineation in auditory environments, coupled with the absence of direct and distinct visual information from other performers, is highlighting a need in change of performative listening; it is urging the performers to seek new ways of adapting, and possibly even altering his auditory balance (where to turn to, what to listen to?)[6]. This implies that in the network, listening needs to become closer to a *sonic flânerie*, in which our ear is urged to be less static; it is asked to reach across nodes, rendering listening more akin to a constant zooming-in and -out of specific sonic images at the different nodes. Performers in the network are simultaneously in an optical auditory space, a distinct, distant and sonically less identifiable space where the sound object/the other performers are distant and remote. At the same time, performers are in a haptic, an intimate and embodied listening space highly familiar to the trained musician. A constant move between optic and haptic listening is demanded of the network performer and the listener/audience alike. In analogy to Deleuze's and Guattari's optic and haptic visuality and in particular with view to the combinatory possibilities and the mixtures of these visualities, musicians in the network are faced with the need to move between two listening attitudes, between optic and haptic, that is, distant and close, delineated and intimate, types of listening.

Indeed, musicians tend to be particularly well equipped to create a continuum between this dialectic, between the two types of listening spaces. Through continuous engagement with their instruments, musicians have developed a particularly intimate relationship with their tools as well as with the sounds they produce. Musicians not only hear in ways that demand minute accuracy, but also they have developed a specific bodily attitude towards their instruments, an embodied way of being with their instruments: the violinist turns her head towards the intimacy of the instrument; she needs to hear-*into*, tune-*into* her instrument. She literally needs to be close to the instrumental body in order to feel and hear the instrument's vibrations. Similarly, the harpist leans forward into her instrument, literally hugging the instrument in order to produce the desired sounds. It is a little less obvious with instruments in which the sound faces away from the performer's body (the clarinet, the trumpet, the oboe etc). Here the physical intimacy with the instrument may not be visually as palpable, but in the same way that the violinist embraces her instrument, the clarinettist endeavours to find this haptic aural space between her body and her instrument. She aurally grabs, re-directs the sound that she emits away from herself in order for the sound to become embodied (re-embodied). Musicians always strive for a haptic aurality. I have argued elsewhere (Schroeder, Rebelo, 2009) that, since performing over the net removes us one level from the others' presence, the performer is urged towards a more intimate being with her body and her instrument, making room for the performer's glances, fantasies and suppositions in an interpretative space.

Steven Connor argues for such intimate disposition of body and instrument when he so poignantly says that one tends to define an instrument “as a sounding posture of the body”, which means that,

> “[w]e learn to hear the postures imprinted in sounds: the fat, farting buttock-cheeks of the tuba, the undulant caressings of the cello. We tend to listen out for the instrument’s manner of production, the mutual disposition of body and instrument that results in the sound” (Connor 2003).

This *sonic flânerie* (the constant move between haptic and optic listening) that I have identified in networked performance environments has clearly opened up new challenges for performers and listeners as well as new definitions of music practice[7], but more interestingly, it has opened up new sounds in themselves. The sonic dynamics of the network are alive and are worth listening to/tuning into: performers now listen to implications of round trip time/delay (RTT), the time which a signal packet takes to travel from the original source to its destination and back and thus we listen to increases and decreases of jitter (network noise), caused by the time variation between packets arriving at their destination (this can be due to network congestion or route changes, for instance). The network has turned technical issues such as latency into musical parameters and thus has led artists to approach technological challenges in more creative ways. Already over ten years ago Atau Tanaka stated that artists tend to,

> “manipulate the technology in a creative manner. The technical limitations become characteristics of the composition. Doing this allows us not to be so worried about transmission delay, rather, to be concerned about the general notion of distance …” (in Bongers, 1998).

Alain Renaud for example plays the network by using latency as musical pulse (Renaud, 2008). The sonic activities at different nodes can indeed become the instruments themselves. In a recent work by composer and digital artist Pedro Rebelo, entitled “Netrooms: The Long Feedback” (2008) the network is made audible by means of the participants’ contributions at the different nodes. In the work, the participants contribute to an extended feedback loop and delay line across the internet. Rebelo states the

> “work explores the juxtaposition of multiple spaces as the acoustic, the social and the personal environment becomes permanently networked. The performance consists of live manipulation of multiple real-time streams from different locations, which receive a common sound source. “Netrooms” celebrates the private acoustic environment as defined by the

> space between one audio input (microphone) and output (loudspeaker)" (Rebelo 2008).

The performance of "Netrooms" is the live mixing of a feedback loop with the signals from each stream. While celebrating the private environment/the local, "Netrooms" also questions the often-assumed notion of the network as being indifferent towards space. In the performance of "Netrooms" as an audience we are allowed access to the spatial and acoustic intimacies of each performer's environment, and notions of distance become problematised. Manuel Castells elaborates on the topology of networks and the distance between nodes, when stating that the

> "topology defined by networks determines that the distance (or intensity and frequency of interaction) between two points (or social positions) is shorter (or more frequent, or more intense) if both points are nodes in a network than if they do not belong to the same network. On the other hand, within a given network, flows have no distance, or the same distance, between nodes. Thus, distance (physical, social, economic, political, cultural) for a given point or position varies between zero (for any node in the same network) and infinite (for any point external to the network)" (Castells, 2000, p501).

Afterthought

It becomes clear that these changes in sounds and concepts about sounds in the network require entirely different listening attitudes. As the walls of our traditional listening spaces (the radio, the walk-men, the ipod, the CD player, or the mobile phone) become turned into 'extended remote walls'[8], in network performances our ears are required at two nodes (if not more) simultaneously. We need to listen simultaneously to the optical (the virtual/physically absent) as well as to the haptic (the physically close and bodily intimate). The challenges for performing in the network lie in making room for an intimacy not only with one's instrument and with one's sound, but also, since the performer is asked to become intimate with the mirror of her sound (relayed through the network), with the sound of the disparate instruments, and with the differing acoustics of the other sites.

Don Ihde's statement, "it is to the invisible that listening may attend" (Ihde, 1976, p14), might be re-appropriated when reflecting on network music making to, 'it is *due* to the invisible that listening has become attended to'.

References

Barbosa, Alvaro (2006). *Displaced Soundscapes*. PhD thesis. Department of Technology of the Pompeu Fabra University (for the Program in Computer Science and Digital Communication).

Bongers, Bert (1998). *An interview with Sensorband.* Computer Music Journal 22, 13-24 (1998).

Castells, Manuel. (2000). *The rise of the network society* (2nd ed.). Malden, MA: Blackwell Publishers.

Connor, Steven (2003). *Ears have walls: on hearing art.* (Talk given in the series bodily knowledges: challenging ocularcentricity at Tate Modern). Available: www.bbk.ac.uk/english/skc/earshavewalls [September 2009].

Deleuze, Gilles and Guattari, Félix (1988). *A Thousand Plateaus: Capitalism and Schizophrenia*. Minneapolis: University of Minnesota Press.

Hirsh, Ira (1959). *Auditory Perception of temporal Order*. Journal of the Acoustical Society of America 31, 759-767.

Ihde, Don (1976). *Listening and voice: a phenomenology of sound.* Athens: Ohio University Press.

Marks Laura (2004). *Haptic Visuality: Touching with the eyes.* Available: http://www.framework.fi/2_2004/visitor/artikkelit/marks.html [September 2009]

McGrath, Kimberley; Blachford, Stacey (eds.) (2001). *Gale Encyclopedia of Science Vol. 1*: Aardvark-Catalyst (2nd ed.), Gale Group.

Renaud, Alain and Caceres, Juan-Pablo (2008). Playing the network: the use of time delays as musical devices. Available: http://www.alainrenaud.net/?p=25, [September 2009].

Schroeder, Franziska. et al. (2007). *Addressing the Network: Performative Strategies for Playing Apart.* Proceedings of the 2007 International Computer Music Conference (ICMC), Copenhagen, 133–9. Link to online video documentation: http://www.sarc.qub.ac.uk/pages/net/study. [September 2009].

Schroeder, Franziska and Rebelo, Pedro (2009). *Sounding the Network: The Body as Disturbant.* Leonardo Electronic Almanac, Special Issue: Dispersive Anatomies. Available: http://www.leonardo.info/LEA/DispersiveAnatomies/DispersiveAnatomies.html [September 2009].

Weinberg, Gil (2002). *The Aesthetics, History, and Future Challenges of Interconnected Music Networks.* Proceedings of the International Computer Music Conference 2002.

—. (2005). *Interconnected Musical Networks: Toward a Theoretical Framework.* Computer Music Journal 29, 23-39 (2005).

Wikipedia (2009). *Haptic technology.* Available: http://en.wikipedia.org/wiki/Haptic_technology. [September 2009].

Zuern, John (1988). *Lacan: The Mirror Stage.* Available: http://www.english.hawaii.edu/criticalink/lacan/index.html [September 2009].

Notes

[1] From the Greek "amoibè (αμοιβή)" meaning change (McGrath, 2001).

[2] 'Nomos' in D&G designates a mode of distribution, one without division. 'Nomos' is like nomadic space that distributes people or animals, in an open, an indefinite and noncommunicating space. "The nomos is the consistency of a fuzzy aggregate: it is in this sense that it stands in opposition to the law or the polis, as the backcountry, a mountainside or the vague expanse around a city…" (D&G, 1988, p380).

[3] Lacan designated two "others": the other with a lower case "o", which is the "other" through which the subject in the mirror stage experiences his own "I", an image of the ego as an Ideal-I. The second Other with a capital "O" represents other people, that the individual may encounter in his life (Zuern, 1988).

[4] Heidegger also draws attention to Contemporary philosophy as a thinking routed in a 'showing forth', a vibrant vision of "Being" (Ihde, 1976, p6). The world is dominated by visualism, so Ihde argues, and major thinkers showed preference for vision. Aristotle for example valued sight as the principle source of knowledge (ibid, p7).

[5] There are several writings that discuss issue of real time auditory feedback in network music. See Barbosa, 2008 and Weinberg, 2002/2005 for instance.

[6] A recent study examined various acoustic and visual information, that were deemed to be useful for performers in networked music performance environments (Apart Study: in Schroeder et al. 2007 and online video documentation).

[7] Jason Freeman's definition of networked music embraces "music practice situations where traditional aural and visual connections between participants are augmented, mediated or replaced by electronically-controlled connections" (in Barbosa, 2006, p25).

[8] Jerome Joy live-blogged this rather intriguing phrase during a Netrooms performance on the 11 December 2008: http://netrooms.wordpress.com/2008/12/11/netrooms/#comment-8.

CHAPTER TEN

ZAIREEKA BY THE FLAMING LIPS: AN INTRODUCTION AND SOME IMPLICATIONS

DESMOND TRAYNOR

My purpose, referencing the theme of 'content', particularly user-generated content, interaction and design, is to discuss the concept and implications of the Flaming Lips' 1997 album, *Zaireeka*. I will begin with a general introduction to this work's genesis and reception, and then I will go on to suggest some possible implications of this singular and ground-breaking release.

But first, a little information about the Flaming Lips. They are a band from Oklahoma City, formed in 1983, who have been through an assortment of line-up incarnations, but since 1996 have coalesced around three core members: founders Wayne Coyne and Michael Ivens, on vocals and occasional guitar, and bass, respectively; and 1993 recruit Steven Drodz, a multi-instrumentalist who joined as a drummer, but now takes care of most of the musicianship in the recording studio, and plays guitar and keyboards in concert. They are supplemented by live drummer Kliph Scurlock. They have released twelve albums thus far, of which 1997's *Zaireeka* was the eighth. In combining elements and tonalities of prog and punk, soul and psyche, particularly since 1999's mainstream breakthrough *The Soft Bulletin*, without this daring genre-mixing sounding like a sonically incompatible Frankenstein's monster, but rather more like some hitherto undiscovered, entirely new fusion, they have as much affinity for melody as for blistering noise assaults.

They are also noteworthy in that as an ostensible 'indie' band, they have been with major label conglomerate Warner Bros., taking advantage of the increased distribution network it affords them, since the recording of their fifth album, 1992's *Hit to Death in the Future Head*, despite only very modest sales for it and for their subsequent three releases: *Transmissions*

From The Satellite Heart (1993), *Clouds Taste Metallic* (1995), and our subject today, *Zaireeka.* They have managed to retain this position, when the relative financial failure of these releases would have them designated as 'flops' by industry standards, by keeping their overheads low and adopting a D.I.Y, thrift store ethic, especially in regard to touring. Despite their critical and commercial successes of the noughties, they remain very hands-on in their approach, setting up and testing their own equipment before performances, and never placing their own gear on stage until supporting bands have finished their sets.

Indeed, to begin focusing more closely on *Zaireeka* itself, the story goes that the general manager at Warner Bros., Jeff Gold, hated the idea of *Zaireeka* being a four-CD set and wanted to drop the band from the label, according to A&R rep, David Katznelson. The Lips' manager, Scott Booker, needed all his business acumen and charm to sell the notion to Steven Baker, who had become president of the label at a time when fearful executives summarily rejected any offbeat and potentially unprofitable idea. Fortunately, Baker's respect for the group's work ethic and resourcefulness helped. He has said: "I was dealing with bands coming to me and saying, 'We need a backdrop that costs ten thousand dollars' or 'We need these lights that cost twenty grand.' I'd be thinking, 'You assholes, look at the Flaming Lips: They have a better light show, and it came from Ace Hardware! Don't you get it? This is your career, and you have to do it yourself.'"[1] I will return later to the economics of getting the album released.

As mentioned, *Zaireeka* is a four-disc package, but the four CDs are not primarily intended to be listened to individually or sequentially (although they certainly can be). Rather, different elements of the same song compositions have been separated and reproduced on the different discs, requiring that the four discs be played simultaneously on four different stereo systems, with the eight individual tracks synchronised at the start by way of band count-ins on the different discs ("1" on disc one, "2" on disc two, etc). Between combining the discs (i.e. in groups of two, three or four) and toying with volume, balance, fidelity, bass, treble, speaker position etc., on four different reproduction sources, the options and possibilities for how listeners hear the songs are truly limitless, or certainly exceed those offered by the conventional two speaker stereo set up. (And it is usually 'listeners' rather than 'listener', since unless you cheat stated authorial intentions by using pre-programmed staggered starts for each CD, properly synchronized multi-disc playback requires more than one person to turn on the four machines at the same time, so it is literally a 'party' album.) Furthermore, no two multi-disc listening experiences of the work can be repeated, thanks to the space-time continuum and discrepancies in speed from one CD player to another. Musically as well as conceptually, the Lips are defiantly experimental throughout *Zaireeka*. Individually, each disc sounds more like free jazz than pop, although Wayne Coyne's melodic sensibilities prevail even during the most chaotic moments. With each additional disc, though, the music's force and ingenuity reveals itself.

Where did the idea for this extravagant opus come from? The title is a combination of the words 'Zaire' and 'Eureka', a term coined by Coyne, as it were, to symbolise the fusion of anarchy and genius. In the album's liner notes, he explains:

> "One day while on tour in Europe somewhere we were driving and listening to the news of the day on the radio. I remember a newscaster with a British accent saying these ominous words: 'Civilization as we know it is breaking down at a phenomenal rate.' He was talking about Zaire, you know, in Africa. And I thought to myself, what if we were actually driving around and playing shows in Zaire instead of Europe... What would you play to an audience whose civilization was "breaking down??"...Since then, to me the word "Zaire" has always been synonymous with "trouble." And it made me think that people who have touted the idea of "anarchy" as the ultimate solution obviously have never really experienced it.' He continues: 'So anyway it's Zaire fused with Eureka - *Zaireeka*!! Both of these spheres of thought happening at exactly the same time - a kind of progress because of decline - simultaneously - but instead of one cancelling out the other - one uses the other. Anarchy using inspiration to guide it. And inspiration using anarchy's abandon and power to crash through any road blocks... whatever that means??... But somewhere in there is the spark that, I think, holds this concept and these songs together..." [2]

Conceptually, the project had its origins in the Parking Lot Experiments, a series of happenings begun in autumn 1996, where the group would distribute thirty different cassettes with a different pre-recorded part to thirty different drivers with their cars arranged in a gigantic circle in a parking lot. The drivers would then load them into their tape decks, roll down their windows, turn up the volume to maximum level, and simultaneously hit play when instructed. Like many of the Flaming Lips' wildest ideas, this one had started simply enough.

In 1978, a seventeen-year-old Coyne had wandered through the parking lot of the Lloyd Noble Center in Norman, Oklahoma before a concert by KISS and Uriah Heep, and noticed the strange effect of different cars blasting the same tune on different eight-track players at the same time. Coyne has said:

> "This led to the idea that we could have all these separate entities playing this big piece of music. I'm doing a weird step that's outside of what we normally know as listening. You can have this enormous sound of a live orchestra, but eventually everything gets reduced to coming out of the left and right speakers. There are other ways to hear things, and that's what I'm playing with. I don't know if I can make it happen, or even if it will be worth listening to if it does happen, but I'm gonna try it." [3]

Coyne expands on this, again in the liner notes:

> "With each experiment I was more encouraged - and even though it had its limitations, I was discovering the possibilities of using separate sound sources to expand on the ideas of composing and listening. And at the same time I was finding that the audience liked the idea of participating in their own entertainment... it was from this process, these failures and successes, that this four CD concept came into being. Though not the same compositions, much of the same ideas are used. My initial recordings of the 'parking lot' things were, I was finding out, dull and flat compared to the way they really sounded. I was finding that the multiple dimensions of having separate sound sources is what gave the compositions their dynamics. What I mean is, when I took a composition that came out of just two speakers right in front of you, well... it was kind of boring, so I set out to see if I could capture the 'unstructuredness' and 'unexpected' elements of what was going on out in the parking lot and put it into a format that could be played in someone's living room... The way the parking lot compositions/performances were fused with a 'multi-dimensional' dynamic is what I would try to do to songs and the recording process. What I mean is... I wanted to abandon song structure but not abandon the song. I wanted to make songs that were different every time you played them. I wanted to veer away from even the way songs were listened to... I wanted to get away from the things that were... known." [4]

With Parking Lot Experiment No. 4 at the eleventh South by Southwest Music and Media Conference, held in Austin, Texas in March 1997, the group played a show unlike any of the other four hundred and ninety-nine performances there, claiming a place in the lineage of avant-garde sonic pioneers stretching from Karlheinz Stockhausen, who wrote a string quartet to be played from four helicopters, to John Cage, of the famously doctored pianos.

Of course, *Zaireeka* is not the first attempt at reproducing sound or music through more than two channels. In the early fifties, American cinemas were utilising a variety of systems stemming from the development of "binaural sound", or "stereo" as it is popularly called, in the thirties, most with four but some with as many as seven channels. When 'high fidelity' audio equipment arrived in homes a few years later, it employed only two channels because phonograph records at the time could not accommodate more sonic information. In the early seventies, improvements in the manufacturing of vinyl LPs led to the birth of quadraphonic sound. When one of the Flaming Lips' major influences, Pink Floyd, recorded their 1973 album *Dark Side of the Moon*, they mixed it for four speakers. Pink Floyd had been playing with the idea in concert for years, since its live-sound engineers developed the fancifully named Azimuth Coordinator, a joystick device that they manipulated to move the music coming from the stage between speakers surrounding listeners in each corner of the hall. Unfortunately, competitive audio manufacturers could never agree on a standard format for quadraphonic sound, which confused and frustrated consumers, who failed to embrace it. But the four-channel concept returned in the early eighties with the advent of home theatre equipment and surround sound.

Even so, with quadraphonic sound and surround sound, there is still only one source, leaving less room for listener participation in the process of listening. In 1996, the Flaming Lips knew that relatively few of their fans owned high-end audiophile gear, but everyone seemed to have more than one CD player: the conventional stereo-system component, augmented by a computer player or perhaps a boom box or two. Coyne began talking with longstanding band producer Dave Friedmann about how listeners might duplicate the multisource sonic swirl of the Parking Lot Experiments at home in a simple and low-tech way. Initially, Coyne hoped to release ten CDs designed to be played simultaneously, but manager Booker, who faced the challenge of packaging the music so that Warner Bros. could sell it, and Friedmann, who had to record the daunting multidisc epic, prevailed upon him to settle for the more realistic number of four.

The group started recording in April 1997 at Tarbox Road Studios in Cassadaga, upstate New York, which Dave Friedmann had just opened. Michael Ivens joined him in tearing out, rewiring, and re-configuring much of the equipment he had just installed, rigging a system to record and mix four separate stereo masters at once. The group recorded on two eight-track ADAT (Alesis Digital Audio Tape) machines running in conjunction with the twenty-four-track analogue tape machine, then mixed to four stereo DAT machines wired to eight speakers.

Solving the technological problems proved to be easier than creating music that justified all of this trouble. After three months at Tarbox Road, the band had spent half of the budget Warner Bros. had allotted for their next "real" album without completing a single song for its arty side project. The musicians gradually discovered that instead of imposing the four-CD format on its usual songwriting, they had to write specifically for the new medium. This realisation precipitated an outpouring of songs. Not all of them fitted the experimental sonic requirements of *Zaireeka*, but those that took shape as more traditional song forms were earmarked for the next conventional album. By August, eight tracks had been completed for *Zaireeka*, as well as several lushly orchestrated pop songs, including 'Race for the Prize', which wound up as the opener on *Zaireeka*'s successor, *The Soft Bulletin*.

In the tradition of *4'33'* by John Cage, which employed four minutes and thirty-three seconds of silence to shift listeners' attention from the stage and prompt them to hear the ambient sounds around them, and *Metal Machine Music*, the 1975 album by Lou Reed which featured four vinyl LP sides of grating feedback, *Zaireeka* is partly an inspired audio experiment, and partly Situationist, media culture event chutzpah. Hints of the gorgeous sounds that would flower on *The Soft Bulletin* can be heard on four of the eight songs, and these do work as conventional stereo mixes, though there are certainly added dimensions in the eight-speaker format.

'Riding to Work in the Year 2025 (Your Invisible Now)' is a hook-laden, multipart orchestral suite with lyrics that tell one of Wayne Coyne's science-fiction tales: a secret agent tries to stop a plot to end the world but ends up "reporting back to nothing" when his headquarters is destroyed. A similarly dire story unfolds in 'Thirty-Five Thousand Feet of Despair', a haunting tune with symphonic flourishes, concerning an anxious pilot who commits suicide in mid-air.

The group revisits familiar terrain with the other two so-called "conventional" tracks, 'A Machine in India' and 'The Big Ol' Bug Is the New Baby Now.' Based on an acoustic guitar decorated by Steven's synthesised flute, the melody of the former owes much to Big Star's 'The

India Song'. In the liner notes, Coyne explains that the lyrics stemmed from a conversation he had with his partner, Michelle Martin, "about the 'other world' she is in during her menstrual period and the kind of dull and depressing mild insanity that seems to possess her." The story-song 'The Big Ol' Bug Is the New Baby Now' pairs a musical coda with Coyne's spoken-word account of how the couple's three dogs adopted a plastic grasshopper that they treated as if it were their offspring, sparing it the fate of being chewed to death. The track ends with an audio assault of barking dogs.

The remaining four tracks exist to showcase the eight-speaker format, and they really cannot be appreciated fully unless you take the trouble of arranging four CD players. If you do, sounds zip around the room, weird noises erupt from unexpected places, and unlikely melodies come together and mutate in bizarre ways. 'Okay I'll Admit That I Really Don't Understand' is a one-chord drone over which Coyne repeats the title, mantra-like; 'The Train Runs Over the Camel But Is Derailed By The Gnat' combines three unrelated melodies and a swirl of ambient noise; 'March of the Rotten Vegetables' is Drodz's electronically doctored drum solo, in the style of Pink Floyd's 'A Saucerful of Secrets', from the Parking Lot Experiments; and 'How Will We Know (Futuristic Crashendos)' is distinguished by high and low-frequency drones. "Can cause a person to become disorientated, confused, or nauseated" caution the liner notes. "Make sure infants are out of listening range. This track should not be listened to while driving." [5]

Having completed the album, how did the Lips convince their label Warner Bros. to release it? Their manager Scot Booker carefully crafted his pitch: for an advance of two hundred thousand dollars, they would deliver two albums, the experimental *Zaireeka*, which it would not count as one of the seven albums required by its contract, and the next pop disc. He also had an answer prepared for why *Zaireeka* should be released first, arguing that most reviews of the band's work up until then, even if conceding that they had some good songs, tended to stress their weirdness. Booker believed that if *Zaireeka* appeared first, everyone would get tired of calling them weird, get it out of their systems, leaving them open to focusing instead on the musical content of the next record.

A week before meeting with Warner Bros' president, Steven Baker, Booker worked his way through every department at the label, collecting the figures to bolster his case. He did his homework as regards manufacturing costs, packaging options and distribution. He calculated that if *Zaireeka* sold twelve thousand copies Warner's would break even, and start making money after that. Warner's were sceptical of even selling that amount, but then advance orders came in for fourteen thousand. So the album was released as a specially priced boxed set in October 1997.

It did not win the band any new fans, garner any radio play, or broach the charts, but supporters held listening parties at rock clubs and record shops across the United States, generating a deal of 'Aren't they weird?' press coverage, as Booker had predicted. To date, *Zaireeka* has sold over twenty-eight thousand copies, more than double the number the record company needed to turn a profit.

The Flaming Lips also devised a novel way of touring in support of their oddest album. Starting in February 1998 and continuing until autumn of that year, following on from the previously discussed precursor to *Zaireeka*, the Parking Lot Experiments, the band brought the Boom Box Experiments to midsized rock clubs across America and Europe, travelling with forty portable cassette players and forty tapes for each song on the set list. The musicians corralled friends and fans in each city to sit on stage in two groups with the boom boxes in their laps. Wayne Coyne conducted the twenty operators on the right, instructing them to raise or lower the volume at different points in each tune, while Steven Drodz directed the twenty on the left, leaving Michael Ivens to stand in the centre, manipulating a mixer that fed lines from all the boom boxes into the house PA, thus producing aleatory songs and soundscapes.

It remains to discuss the appeal of *Zaireeka*, and to suggest why it can be regarded as a significant artistic statement rather than as a monumental folly, or even a noble failure. While working on the album before its release, Wayne Coyne stated that he had two goals for *Zaireeka*, apart from the obvious one of offering another way of hearing music. One was to create a group listening experience; the other was to illustrate the unexpected pleasures of what Brian Eno calls "happy accidents". [6] In terms of these objectives, the work succeeds admirably, on its own terms. *Zaireeka* represents a challenge to the reigning assumptions behind the idea of recorded music and its reproduction, and is an attempt to change the way listeners use the available technology. The open and interactive nature of the project, and the artistic practice which facilitated it, has a direct bearing on user-centred interaction, in which the object that is the means of (re)production – the CD – requires a new species of environment, in terms of listening conditions, for its consumption and appreciation. *Zaireeka* achieves its purposes, I would argue, in three main ways: by being social, by being variable, and by being transient.

Perhaps the most significant facet of this enterprise is that *Zaireeka* almost dictates the conditions of its listening, in that it must be set up through group cooperation and listened to in a social context. Although it is technically possible to synch the tracks by, for example, pausing one CD player after six seconds of play, another after four seconds of play and another after two, and then pressing play on the fourth, counting "one, two" and pressing play on the one paused after two seconds, then counting "three, four" and pressing play on the one paused after four seconds and so on, this method of being able to listen alone (and, so to say, 'cheat' the intentions implicit in the format) misses the spirit of *Zaireeka*. As already mentioned, listening parties became popular in the wake of the album's release, and not just in public premises but also in private homes. A regular topic of the Flaming Lips' mailing list and message boards was *Zaireeka* parties. People were constantly organising them, inviting people to them, and giving reports on how they went afterwards. Few people have four CD players, but most people, if they are lucky, have at least three friends or acquaintances, or friends of friends and acquaintances of acquaintances. Some of these people are bound to own boomboxes. *Zaireeka* provides a great reason to bring people together to listen to music communally. Indeed, a cursory YouTube search will yield documentary evidence of people listening to different tracks from the work at gatherings in apartments, and even an amusing demonstration of how the CDs should be set up.

Similarly, while it is possible with certain software programmes to create a burned, mixed-down version of *Zaireeka*, where the contents of all four CDs can be heard simultaneously on one disc (an understandable desire if the listener wants to focus on the songs and listen to them repeatedly in an easy manner) the only way to think of a *Zaireeka* mixdown is as a souvenir of the real thing. For *Zaireeka* is essentially a multi-disc experience, because it is intended that you will never hear the same record twice, and that every listening experience will be variable, thus more closely approximating a live concert than conventional CD reproduction and listening. Synchronization is the most obvious mitigating factor here. Perfect synchronization is virtually impossible, so each listening experience will vary according to how well you can get the discs to work together. In making a mix-down copy of *Zaireeka*, it is important to remember that each track should be synched separately. The record is not meant to be heard in one long session, as the speeds of CD players are too inconsistent. Once one track ends, it is advisable to pause the CD and start synchronising anew.

But other factors inevitably have a significant impact on each experience. How loud can you play the record? Four stereos going in one room can make quite an impact, even at modest volume. Which disc are you going to assign to your main stereo? The most powerful drum parts occur on disc four, so do you give that one to whichever system has the most bass? And sometimes you can only get three CD players together, which means you have to decide which disc to leave out. The songs remain the same, but the listeners' experiences do not.

In this way, it can be seen that *Zaireeka*'s variability is attained by a meeting and mixing of methods partly controlled and partly aleatory, that is, partly dictated by the necessities attendant on all experiences of listening to pre-recorded sounds, and partly as the result of chance elements occasioned by how this CD package interacts with the available technology. As its title suggests, it is the fusion of the *modus operandi* of an inspiring idea with the anarchy and chaos of random improvisation. Furthermore, *Zaireeka* tends to collapse, or at least to highlight and so challenge, the form/content dichotomy. Is the audience listening because of, and more engaged by, the songs themselves, or by the way they have been recorded and are being reproduced? In this way, *Zaireeka* throws into sharp relief more common debates around musical composition *vis-à-vis* production values on "normal" CDs.

Finally, because of the organisational hassles associated with the social aspect of the work, and more especially because of the variability of each listening experience, there is a transient quality not only to the experience of hearing *Zaireeka*, but to the work itself. It is a collection of pieces of recorded music which tends to inspire the same feelings and reactions as does music in live performance. Conscious of the infrequency with which they may with ease hear the work, and also certain that they will never hear it in precisely the same way ever again, listeners are far less likely to talk over the sound during *Zaireeka* listening parties, and much more apt to listen attentively and with unusual concentration. So, *Zaireeka* attempts to stand outside the canon of recorded music by refusing to be fixed and finished. The paradox being, of course, that this very transience is what contributes to its standing the test of time, and makes it lasting.

It may be asked, why has no one else taken up the gauntlet thrown down by *Zaireeka*? Well, in some ways they have. In the twelve years since its release, advances in technology and more ready access to those advances mean that the *Zaireeka* project is being continued by other means. Apart from the fact that the proliferation of laptops in the intervening period has meant that listening parties are somewhat easier to organise than they were when stereo systems and boom boxes had to be transported to agreed locations, it is also noteworthy that the spread of information technology has given rise to more recent innovations in the composer/audience interface. For example, the band Radiohead have created the opportunity, via their website, for fans to remix already released versions of their songs. Some of these remixes have subsequently been officially released by the band as alternative versions, or made available to download. Nine Inch Nails have also done the same thing. So, while *Zaireeka* remains, as an artefact, *sui generis*, its application and influence is still evolving. But even if it is perceived as a one-off, never to be repeated statement, it can stand its ground as a point that needed to be made, and was sufficient to make only once.

Notes

1. DeRogatis, Jim. *Staring At Sound: The True Story of Oklahoma's Fabulous Flaming Lips.* New York: Broadway, 2006. p.163.

2 The Flaming Lips. *Zaireeka.* Warner Bros., 1997. Liner notes, p.1 ff.

3 DeRogatis, p.151.

4 The Flaming Lips, p.5 ff.

5 The Flaming Lips, p.10.

6 Derogatis, p.162.

CHAPTER ELEVEN

CONTENT AND DISCONTENT

SIMON WATERS

If Duchamp's *Fountain* (1917) teaches us anything it is surely that distinctions between the object and its context - between 'content' and 'container'- are difficult to sustain. And McLuhan, writing in 1964, flags this insight most explicitly in his celebrated formulation: 'the medium is the message'. Nevertheless much activity, particularly in the digital domain, proceeds as if this distinction were self-evident: as if content were in some way a distinct category.

Of course such categories are important to us because the activities of gathering (collecting), discriminating (sorting) and ordering (cataloguing) are fundamental cognitive processes. It is little surprise therefore that the notion of archiving has blossomed, in both scale and scope, since the advent of digital storage and recall.

The archive has come to function as one of the crucial current sites where an archivist's sense of 'content' as a benign category, and of archiving as a relatively dispassionate activity, comes into contention with a perhaps more playful or critical sense of 'archiving' as an essential and inevitable strategy of art making or broader signifying practice.

This short paper looks, from a practitioner's perspective, at the manner in which critically rethinking the relationship between content and container (or simply refusing the distinction altogether) has been, in the broadest sense, aesthetically productive, particularly in highly-technologised environments. Some of these observations are neither very new, nor very profound, but they are gathered here in order to identify certain effects which may be regarded as resulting from their combined cultural impact. In the spirit of the title I draw freely here on my previous writings and presentations - both published (Waters, 2000a/b; 2003) and unpublished - quoting, paraphrasing and refashioning.

I think it is first worth revisiting the notions of gathering, discriminating and ordering (collecting, sorting and cataloguing) to which I referred above, not least because these 'doing' words draw our attention to a crucial, and crucially overlooked aspect of content, which is that it is not an atemporal category of objects with inherent value, but a situated, temporal and processual category determined by the contingencies of active participants.

I'm drawn here to the now unfashionable writing of Gregory Bateson (1972) in which he makes useful distinctions between data (uncontextualised input) and information (data which makes a difference). By implication this latter is data which makes a difference *to* someone or something: a term therefore integrating at some level the process of interpretation, or at least of evaluation. Bateson's notion of information as 'a difference which makes a difference' is based on a the persuasive argument that 'state change' is hardwired in human perceptual systems as 'significance': that steady-state input (visual, aural or whatever) does not constitute 'rich' data and is therefore put into abeyance in our allocation of attention. This has obvious aesthetic implications for a practitioner. 'Minimal' temporal phenomena may, for example, result in two responses: a dulling of attention, or, in some cases, a remapping of the dynamic range of that attention such that small deviations - minute state changes - are refactored as 'significant'. Composers and sound artists are aware of the crucial importance of the 'attack': the first few milliseconds of any sound event, in which the complexities and instabilities of the physical system being excited are at their most potent, and from which we unpack most of the significant identifying detail, and of the consequence that quite different instrumental sounds with their attacks removed can be surprisingly difficult to identify.

But this is a digression. My purpose here is to look at a series of categories which between them suggest at least a couple of hundred years of challenges to and problematisations of the notion of content, particularly in its manifestation as benign, universally accessible information. It is perhaps no surprise that these align historically with pressures for the construction of the modern individual above all as *efficient*, and particularly as efficiently productive and communicative.

The categories I'd like to address are: noise and resolution; overload; supplement; arbitrariness and mutability; emergence; collaboration, authorship and ownership; and silence and absence. In some way they form an interlinked sequence of concerns, all of which I have been forced to confront in my own practice, and I have occasionally drawn upon this, and the work of colleagues, students and other practitioners for illustration.

Noise in the system

Noise is now sufficiently well theorised (by e.g. Kahn, 1999; Hegarty, 2008) whether as a feature of all technologised means of dissemination: an intervention in the 'signal', or (more politically explicitly) as a channelling of informational dissent: Attali's noise as transmuted violence (1985). The aestheticisation of noise is a key trope of modernist practitioners, whether in the polemics of Marinetti and Russolo or, more prosaically, in the increasing crucial role of percussion in the modernist musical vocabulary. Some manifestations of noise art flag their historical specificity by explicit reference to the industrial, Arsenij Avraamov's utilisation of the entire Russian Black Sea fleet as 'orchestra' (cited in Kahn & Whitehead, 1993) being an extreme case in point. Others function as a form of 'heckling', enlisting the strategies of a practice to comment upon and critique it, as in John Oswald's extraordinary and often hilarious *Plunderphonics*[1] or much of Bob Ostertag's work[2].

Long before punk, noise and distortion formed part of the expressive vocabulary of pop music, and it is unsurprising therefore that it should have been in pop music (understood in the broadest sense) that a reaction to the smooth professional surface which digital technology allowed in both image and sound should have emerged most convincingly. This concern with the signifying possibilities of noise, dirt and distortion is given an additional discursive dimension (analogous to the spatial - to direction, or proxemics) in the digital world of high resolution, extended dynamic range and enhanced spectral clarity, by the introduction of a continuum of **resolution** from distorted to clear reproduction, from deliberately compressed or reduced dynamic or spectral range to 'professional' polish. As an expressive device this continuum has been well used by artists who emerged from the Bristol club scene in the early 1990s, notably Tricky and Portishead, and was rapidly adopted by practitioners in electroacoustic music around the same time.

This continuum is articulated partly through the collision of digital 'hi-tech' technologies with resolutely 'lo-tech' solutions to musical problems, and with the profusion of (often simultaneous) formats. Many artists adopt 'lo-tech' approaches as part of an explicit political agenda: avoiding implication in 'corporate' music making by utilising turntables, garage electronics and cheaply available (often deliberately archaic) domestic music technology. Such issues, along with a pragmatic economic sense, inform the use of turntables as performance devices in the urban subculture of the US in the 1980s, and their use by experimental musicians (Christian Marclay, Philip Jeck[3]) intent on drawing attention to the medium of the recording. A typical electroacoustic work from the 1990s, Ed Kelly and Nick Melia's *Block Groove*[4] uses shellac, vinyl and digital recordings and the interventions, treatments and 'degradations' characteristic of all three, to construct a piece in which there is play between an 'acousmatic' sensibility, the performed interventions, and intrusions from the material support of the recording which frequently emerge as 'content'. This might be interpreted here as a deliberate McLuhanesque signalling of the mode of representation, of the means of encoding, as inseparable from 'what is represented'. New York composer Jonathan Mitchell's *Vinyl*[5] and Californian Matt Ingalls's *(f)Ear*[6] are other explorations of similar territory. In mainstream activity one need look no further than Madonna, whose video for *Don't Tell Me* (2000) foregrounds technologies of representation by featuring the singer astride a bucking bronco in an image, initially 'clear' - and read as 'real', which becomes striated by the horizontal transmission lines of NTSC encoding as we zoom towards it. In as further 'nesting' of the modes of representation we then pan out to reveal that all of the image thus far has been reproduced on a huge multiple screen in the desert, and that 'reality', as we knew all along, has even greater resolution.

The sampling paradigm is never far away here - the assumption that all 'content' is mutable - and it is significant that although digital technology afforded the potent instance of a recording device *designed* to function as a performing tool, the archivist's fascination with gathering, discriminating and ordering, and the practitioner's with recontextualising and refashioning, are as evident in the 'beat mining' and 'crate digging' for rare vinyl, as in instant online downloads. Debord's *détournement* [7]- subversion through appropriation - is figured as clearly in early Rap and Hip-Hop as in the work of John Oswald.

Overload: The 'rate of information' problem

A paper by German communications theorist Norbert Bolz, 'The Deluge of Sense' (1994) flags sensory overload as a characteristic of 'modern' life, drawing attention to the 'inhuman velocity' of the transmission of information. Bolz is adamant that:

> the flood of information does not imply knowledge. Mass communication does not provide orientation. *The deluge of sense does not make sense.* On the contrary: the exposure to stimuli of information overload is strongest and most fascinating if the recipient is not able to make use of it. (Bolz, 1994: 1)

One might add that the density and texture of that information may be as significant as its speed, and that a concern with rapid 'channel-switching', perpetually exposing the cognitive system to state-changes hard-wired to provoke response has become one of the most pervasive aesthetic strategies of the late-twentieth and early twenty-first centuries.

'Glitch' and 'flicker' have become genres in themselves, playing on the limits of perceptual stability, foregrounding the resulting ambiguities, disjunctures and instabilities. A concern with 'content' *per se* is replaced by a concern for perceptual 'effect', the work of Liam Wells[8] being a case in point.

This flagging of the medium of delivery or storage as equal in significance to any putative content is in itself a form of noise. As a dystopian, rupturing mechanism it can sometimes (as with reduced, minimal input, as remarked above) provoke paradoxical responses, in that the deluge of sense may afford a rescaling of sensory input, such that both affect and effect are dulled. As a composer of electroacoustic music I have often noted that 'dramatic' spatialisations of movement or direction of sound through multi-loudspeaker 'diffusion' systems serve for many audience members to impair other aspects of their critical listening and enjoyment. Rapid spatial and directional change in sound is hard-wired to 'potential threat', and repeated utilisation of such strategies in music may simply dull the senses.

David Liddle, speaking at the same conference as Bolz (above) notes poignantly that:

> Information has become a real pain. We are saturated with it. It is not the thing that is scarce any longer. The two scarce commodities are attention

> and trust ... [In future] our problem will not be the availability of information, it will be how do we choose to allocate our attention, that's the scarce resource. We only have 16-18 hours a day in which to do anything and allocating our attention is hard. The basis for allocating our attention in my view will be trust, and by trust I don't mean as to whether or not information is accurate, I mean as to whether or not information is relevant or worthwhile or interesting. (Liddle, 1994: 4)

Liddle continues by advancing a compelling argument for the importance of sound in the establishment of 'attention' and 'trust'. Our capacity to selectively 'stream' attention to multiple strands of audio, and the fact that we cannot entirely mute the input, give sound a uniquely demanding quality: an omnipresence celebrated in, for example, Attali's (1985) attribution of such significance to the sonic domain.

Supplement

Even as we engage with activities which might, tolerably in some circumstances, be regarded as productive of 'content', such as playing the trumpet, we engage simultaneously and inevitably in the production of 'supplementary' activity. Of course the distinction between content and supplementarity is usually one of convention or habit, and reductive of the rich affordances of the activity. In digital systems any data stream is simultaneously data, and a potential controller.

Jonathan Impett's *Metatrumpet* (Impett, 1994) involves a series of sensors[9] attached to a concert instrument, running through an interface to a lap-top computer. The sensors allow the harnessing of continuous streams of'data (the performer's position, the angle of the instrument, the patterns of valve use) which is a by-product of the activity of playing the trumpet. This data is harnessed as input for a complex of real-time digital interventions in and developments of the instrument's sound. Every aspect of the work emerges as a result of the interaction between live performance activity and the emergent, complex system behaviour. The project is characterised by Impett's insistence that the data streamed from the sensors is a supplementary component of an *existing* musicianliness. In (Impett, 2001: 108) he describes thus the development of this model for interactive music, which he defines as 'music instantiated in real-time on the basis of local performance and environmental information: Music is understood as a dynamical complex of interacting situated embodied behaviours. These behaviours may be physical or virtual, composed or emergent, or of a time scale such that they figure as constraints or constructs. All interact in the same space by a process of mutual modelling, redescription, and emergent restructuring'. What becomes clearly evident here is the importance of describing such dynamical systems in terms of **behaviour** rather than content.

Arbitrariness and mutability

The notion of content is marked by intentionality, and by being in some sense revisitable or repeatable in order that it might be referenced. But, as suggested above, the essence of sampling is equally of **mutability**: of the capacity to refashion relationships between elements and strands of activity in real time.

An interface conceived around access to 'content' would have identifiably different design criteria from one which afforded more dynamically-conceived behaviour. In a 'content-driven' model a physical action - the movement of a fader, perhaps - must operate according to principles of predictability (a given input producing the same effect each time), linearity (or some similar 'scaling') mapping the physical input to its effect, and stability (the global behaviour of the device remaining fixed). But such design principles may be hugely reductive of the potential behaviours afforded by a similar device - another fader - which is characterised by travel in which there is a dynamically-determined point at which one behaviour flips over into another, or in which there are significant breaks and deviations from linearity in the relationship between input gesture and effect. Most of all if the entire function of the device gradually remaps over time the nature of engagement afforded becomes necessarily dynamic: decisions have to be made 'in the moment'. The work of researchers such as John Bowers (Bowers & Hellström, 2000; Bowers, 2003) on interface design and improvising machines is particularly valuable here.

Once behaviour is identified as a more appropriate concern than content, the question of the agency of that behaviour emerges. Collecting, sorting, cataloguing and searching activities are now subject to algorithmic intervention to various degrees, and as these cognitive categories are as fundamental to e.g. composing as to archiving, it is inevitable that a practitioner's role increasingly involves devolving tasks to software 'agents'. These may 'behave' in a manner entirely determined by the human agent, or they may exhibit varying degrees of independence and dynamic development. In some cases the result may be that collecting, sorting, and cataloguing are devolved to a dynamic ‘feature-matching’ function in which the responsiveness of a computer agent to input from a performer ‘feels like’ the presence of another human agent, featuring both ‘appropriateness’ and apparent ‘arbitrariness’ in its repertoire. The work of David Plans Casal with Michael Casey’s *Soundspotter*[10] real-time audio matching tools (e.g. Casal & Morelli, 2007) is, to my knowledge, the most consistently developed practitioner-driven investigation of this area of activity, calling upon Casal’s considerable and well-matched abilities as concert pianist and programmer in the development of ‘somebody’ fast, technically-able, and ‘imaginative’ with whom the human performer may improvise ‘on demand’.

The Virtual/Physical-Feedback (VPFI) flute[11] represents my own attempt to model and explore the relationship between the bodily and the virtual in a personally comprehensible manner: to make sense out of multiple streams of data notably with respect to ‘foundness’ or ‘unforeseenness’ in performance. Such qualities are regarded as creating particular difficulties in digitally-mediated contexts in which sustaining ‘attention’ is problematic, but ‘forgetting’ is also paradoxically difficult. The system’s embracing of the arbitrary reconnects us with Bateson, who develops his argument (Bateson, 1975) by suggesting that, if information is difference which makes a difference, the fundamental source of ‘the new’ is therefore randomness or arbitrariness.

The current VPFI flute system involves acoustic feedback[12], feedback through DSP physical modeling, and feedback through Casey's Soundspotter technology[13] which, in conjunction with an evolving genetic evaluation system (Casal, 2007), contributes 'matching' material from the buffer in a constant and developing dialogue with the player. The proposed next stage of implementation is to extend the system to operate with sound input streamed to Soundspotter from audio searches of the web. This is not merely a technical extension. The current system extends my concern to manifest a model of sonic proxemics, the underpinning concept being that ‘sound is a form of touch’[14]. Self-evidently, the basic acoustic feedback operation of the system, with its immediacy of response to the slightest physical change, is regarded as mapping onto ‘intimate’ space, the DSP and ‘local’ Soundspotter activity represents Hall’s ‘social and consultative’ space, and the web-based input to Soundspotter represents ‘public or environmental’ space. Performance on the system thus affords exploration of both social and sonic aspects of musical space.

Emergence

Complex systems such as that described above can be characterized as having **emergent** properties in the sense that the resulting behaviours do not come about from the operation of a single rule or event but rather from an 'ecology'of interactions between all of the elements in a given environment, and frequently, that environment itself. Composer Agostino Di Scipio is keen to stress what he calls the bio-ecological principles involved in a series of works which he calls *Audible Ecosystemics*, in particular energy exchange, structural closure, organisational openness and structural coupling of system and environment. The works utilise feature extraction within a feedback system consisting of a conjunction of microphones, loudspeakers, computers and rooms, in which feature extraction generates low rate control signals which drive gradual interventions in the sound material. In addition the computer cross-compares microphone input signal and system output, generating difference signals which are also fed back into the system as controls, so the system can be said to develop a sense of its own history - an evolutionary perspective. Di Scipio avoids using the term 'interactive', preferring to describe 'dynamical interdependencies among system components' (Di Scipio, 2003)

Transposed into the social and political domain of the interpretation or reading of a work the term emergent has been appropriated as indicating a conscious utilisation of the changing boundaries between the subject (listener, interpreter) and the maker (artist, composer), in which the former interact with what the latter has made, such that the work can be said to emerge in its 'use', rather than having been designed in its entirety by the artist and then 'presented'. This too might be regarded as a principle enhanced by the mechanisms (technological and social) associated with digital technologies, and a significant challenge to unproblematised notions of content.

Collaboration, authorship and ownership

The notion of content is irrevocably historically intertwined with notions of authorship, ownership and copyright. Authority has been conferred as the result of filtering processes (such as editorship in publishing) which afford 'trust' on the part of those who buy into that content. But digitally-mediated processes for amassing and distributing invite both automated and collaborative contributions and interventions which are far less 'accountable', and this very anonymity has become an important factor in the behaviour of many current practitioners. This increased tendency toward collaborative or collective working may result from the fact that, at least in the (historically) early stages of the forms of work we are considering, artists tended - often out of necessity - to work together with technicians and with programmers, as well as from the fact that the networking possibilities of the physical world are now multiplied so dramatically by networking in the digital domain. Within such collaborative enterprise, the notion of authorship is no longer a necessary condition of a work's emergence, although, as media theorist Andreas Broeckmann has pointed out, 'we should not underestimate the degree to which envy, fame, sex, money and power still play their roles' (Broeckmann, 1996). Some of the collaboration undoubtedly results from the degree of hybridisation between previously separate disciplines or areas of expertise which is encouraged by the increasingly similar interfaces used for manipulation of text, image, sound etc. Some I would ascribe to the physical isolation of screen-based working practices, and can be regarded as a response to that physical isolation: a critique of the inadequacy of the interface between digital devices and analogue human beings which has led to a compensatory re-socialising of the process of making. Finally, and most obviously, the connectivity which results from current networks facilitates and even encourages the likelihood that collaborative activity might result from input at geographically disparate locations. Currently such distributed activity is most successful in situations where temporal synchronisation is not critical: non time-based work or 'ambient' musical activity, and although technically surmountable, the problems associated with dispersed real-time synchronised activity make it most evident in contexts where there is significant institutional support[15].

As I have written elsewhere (Waters, 2000a: 76), the sampler elegantly utilises two of the fundamental characteristics of digital systems: massive non-linear data storage, and the capacity to address that stored data at any point instantly. In doing so it effectively (and by design) blurs the distinction between 'creative' and 'disseminative' technologies, and therefore the distinction between composer and listener. Affording 'users' the capacity to reformulate and refashion material may constitute the most significant challenge to a notion of content. It is significant that even the most seemingly institutionalised practices of archiving and 'curatorship' are replicated in informal social space (e.g. by record collectors, train spotters, DJs etc.) and are increasingly fascinating as aesthetic strategy, Christian Boltanski's work - particularly that addressing notions of memory and forgetting - being illustrative here[16]. The prevalence of 'digital repositories' such as that associated with the Ars Electronica Center in Linz[17] illustrates a delicious irony in that the fluidity and transience which characterise many aspects of digital culture (websites and their addresses, for example - especially illegal download sites - or online multi-site performances) are counterbalanced by immense social and economic pressures to fixity and permanence. Perhaps, in a more critical exploration of the play between these two counterbalancing tendencies, a digital equivalent of the sort of filter system which operated to limit the survival of pre-digital aesthetic production (the cost of publishing and printing books, for example) will emerge as a factor in systems for storage and diffusion.

Silence

A final potent challenge to content comes from the antithesis of noise and overload: **absence** and **silence**. The electroacoustic compositions of Nick Melia[18], for example, operate at the extremes of the perception threshold in both frequency and amplitude. By using primarily extremely high or extremely low frequencies, and sounds which are replayed at or just above the ambient noise level of a particular performance space, the composer inhibits ascription on the part of the listener, approaching a condition in which there is a resistance to or deferral of interpretation. Audience members report carrying 'ghost' frequencies out of the concert hall which sustain 'prosthetically' in the body for many minutes. Another young composer, Stef Edwards[19], who espouses an interest in 'programming for unexpectedness' (to himself) and in 'making a system sufficiently complex that one can't know what will happen' - concerns which link him to the discussion earlier - utilises 'absence' in his project *Radio Pieces*. In this work listeners are encouraged to phone into a radio station while keeping their radios, tuned to the same station, as near to the telephone as possible. The resulting acoustic feedback from the open phone-lines, mixed and balanced by the composer at the radio station as it happens, animates this 'central' space with the influence of the distributed, external spaces occupied by the listeners, providing the 'silent' core with 'content' to broadcast.[20] The social elements, distributedness and emergence, are as significant here as the sonic components. The ecosystem is both sonic and social.

Work and working

The issues listed impinge on aesthetic production not least because a significant factor in any process of aesthetic development is the existence of (one's own) previous work. Beyond the obvious notion of perfectibility - that in each work at some level one hopes to supplant and improve upon the perceived inadequacies of the previous attempt - there is the more mundane fact that each work generates a large proportion of unused material at various stages of development. Within my own work this backlog of unresolved compositional problems has always been reinvested in the subsequent project to some degree, with two inevitable consequences: The first is that the 'status' of material becomes extraordinarily fluid: what might have been a relatively complete musical 'statement' can reappear as a sample source or control strategy for improvisatory inclusion in another work: distinctions between 'source material', 'transformations', and 'completed sections' are contingent only on a particular instance of use. The second is that a degree of continuity is established (at least for the maker) between works which usefully blurs the sometimes arbitrary disjunction of the completion of 'the work' from the ongoing process of 'working'. The very banality of these observations, reified each time I work, is enough to give me pause whenever the notion of 'content' arises.

References

Attali, Jacques (1985). *Noise: The Political Economy of Music* (Manchester: Manchester University Press)

Bateson, Gregory (1972) *Steps to an Ecology of Mind* (Chicago: University of Chicago Press, 1999 edn.)

Bolz, Norbert (1994) 'The Deluge of Sense' *Mediamatic*, vol.8 (Amsterdam, Mediamatic) CD-ROM (transcription of speech at 'Doors of Perception' Conference, Amsterdam 1993.)

Bowers, John and Hellström, Sten-Olof (2000). 'Simple Interfaces to Complex Sound in Improvised Music' CID-95 at: http://cid.nada.kth.se/en/publicat/all.html (Stockholm, Centre for User-Oriented Interface Design)

Bowers, John (2003). 'Improvising Machines: Ethnographically Informed Design for Improvised Electro-Acoustic Music' in *ARiADATexts 4* www.ariada.uea.ac.uk/ariadatexts/ariada4/ariada4_text.html

Broeckmann, Andreas (1996) 'Towards an Aesthetics of Heterogenesis' (Rotterdam, V2 Organisation) at:

http://www.v2.nl/~andreas/texts/1996/aestheticsofheterogenesis.html
Casal, David Plans & Morelli, Davide (2007) 'Remembering the future: applications of genetic co-evolution in music improvisation' *Proceedings of the European Conference on Artificial Life, Lisbon, 2007* available at www.davidcasal.com/wp-content/uploads/2007/05/finaldraft.pdf

Debord, Guy (1967)*The Society of the Spectacle* accessible at http://library.nothingness.org/articles/SI/en/display25

Di Scipio, Agostino (2003)' 'Sound is the Interface': Sketches of a Constructivitic Ecosystemic View of Interactive Signal Processing' *Proceedings of the Colloquium on Musical Informatics, Firenze 8-10 May 2003* (Florence: CIM) at http://xoomer.alice.it/adiscipi/CIM03b.pdf

Hall, Edward T. (1966). *The Hidden Dimension* (New York, Doubleday)

Hegarty, Paul (2008) *Noise/Music: A History* (New York, Continuum)

Impett, Jonathan (1994). 'A meta-trumpet(-er)' in *Proceedings of the International Computer Music Conference* (San Francisco, ICMA)

—. (2001) 'Interaction, simulation and invention: a model for interactive music' in Bilotta, Miranda, Pantano and Todd (eds.) *Artificial Life Models for Music Applications*, pp.108-119. (Cosenza: Bios) also available at http://galileo.cincom.unical.it/esg/Music/workshop/articoli/impett.pdf.

Kahn, Douglas (1999). *Noise, Water, Meat* (Cambridge, MIT)

Kahn, Douglas and Whitehead, Gregory eds. (1993). W*ireless Imagination: Sound, Radio and the Avany-Garde* (Cambridge, MIT)

Liddle, David (1994). 'How the Computer Industry Unfolded and The Beginning of a New Emerging Species' *Mediamatic*, vol.8 (Amsterdam, Mediamatic) CD-ROM (Transcription of speech at 'Doors of Perception' Conference, Amsterdam 1993.)

McLuhan, Marshall (1964). *Understanding Media: The Extensions of Man* (Cambridge, MIT, 1994 edn.)

Renaud, Alain B., Carôt, Alexander and Rebelo, Pedro (2007) 'Networked Music Performance: State of the Art' in *Proceedings of AES30th International Conference,* (Saariselkä, Finland) *2007 March 15-17* available at http://www.livemusicportal.eu/lmp7/images/stories/publications/AES_30_Paper_AR_AC_PR_Final.pdf

Van Alphen, Ernst (2008). Visual Archives and the Holocaust: Christian Boltanski, Ydessa Hendeles and Peter Forgacs' in Van den Braembussche et al. (eds) *Intercultural Aesthetics: A Worldview Perspective* pp137-155 (Springer, Dordrecht)

Waters, Simon (2000a). 'Beyond the acousmatic: Hybrid tendencies in electroacoustic music', in Emmerson, S (ed) *Music, Electronic Media and Culture* (Aldershot, Ashgate)

—. (2000b). 'The musical process in the age of digital intervention', in *ARiADA Texts* 1 (December 2000): http://www.ariada.uea.ac.uk/

—. (2003). 'Thinking the unheard: Hybrid thought in musical practice' in Monks, J. and Gullström-Hughes, R (eds) *Hybrid Thought* (Milton Keynes, Open University)

Notes

[1] http://www.plunderphonics.com/

[2] http://bobostertag.com/

[3]Philip Jeck is best known for his *A Vinyl Requiem* (London, 1993) with Lol Sargent, a performance/installation involving projection from 2 slide- projectors and 2 movie-projectors onto a bank of 180 'Dansette' record players. Works by New York-based Marclay, whose business card apparently describes him as 'record player', are discussed in a 1998 interview at http://www.furious.com/perfect/christianmarclay.html

[4] ARiADA, University of East Anglia, 1999, at http://www.sara.uea.ac.uk/

[5] 1993 – at http://www.prx.org/pieces/3481

[6] 1997 version for tape alone - http://sfsound.org/matt/compositions.html

[7] Debord's concept of détournement is complex and fluid, incorporating notions of (mis)appropriation, of turning aside from something's usual function, of re-use in an unforeseen manner, of deflection, negation and of the inverse of quotation. (Debord, 1967: theses 206-210)

[8] http://www.liamwells.co.uk/vid/water.html

[9] Mercury switches, pressure, ultrasound, Hall-effect, acceleration and breath sensors are used, and pitch to MIDI devices and envelope followers also operate on the acoustic signal.

[10] http://soundspotter.org/

[11] http://musariada.mus.uea.ac.uk/~simon/performance-ecosystem/

[12] A physical system in which the amplified signal from an ordinary acoustic concert flute is replayed through a small loudspeaker and transmission line system back into the body of the flute through a plastic tube inserted through the cork in the headjoint of the instrument.

[13] Using MPEG7 metadata to provide rapid correlation between input signal and real-time analysis of massive buffered audio signals - live or from file.

[14] Proxemics (Hall, 1966) has to do with the definition of personal 'zones' or territories that surround individuals: These are categorised as intimate space, social and consultative or 'local' space, and public or environmental space.

[15] Some of the most consistent research in this area is being coordinated by Alain Renaud - http://www.alainrenaud.net/ and is documented in e.g. Renaud, Carôt and Rebelo, 2007

[16] Boltanski's engagement with archiving is best approached via *La Vie Impossible* (2001) and *Les archives de C.B.* (1965-88, 1989), referenced at http://www.centrepompidou.fr/education/ressources/ENS-Boltanski_en/ENS-Boltanski_en.htm, and is discussed in van Alphen (2008)

[17] http://www.aec.at/

[18] http://www.sara.uea.ac.uk/

[19] http://www.sara.uea.ac.uk/

[20] *Radio Pieces* was first broadcast in June 2002 by Resonance FM, a limited coverage London-based station.

CHAPTER TWELVE

BREAKING THE MAGIC CIRCLE

DANE WHITE

> Games are not a kind of cinema, or literature, but colonizing attempts from both these fields have already happened, and no doubt will happen again. And again, until computer game studies emerges as a clearly self-sustained academic field.
> —Aarseth, 2001

Video games are one of the most successful entertainment industries in the world today, but unlike other entertainment mediums like cinema or music it is often not discussed as an art form. Within the discussion of the medium itself video games are generally not viewed as art, nor even capable of being seen as art. Perhaps this lack of artistic discussion is due to the fact that video games are a form of new media and as such are approached differently than other mediums. Can a highly mutable medium be seen as art and how would this be different than other art forms so as to warrant particular study? How would this art form be helpful to theory and conceptions of art? If games are a new media, then it is that quality that separates games from old media and other media theories that allow games to be defined as a separate medium, and it is upon this quality that games can be seen as an art form. Using gameplay, which for me is the fundamental characteristic that separates games from other media, I will explore how designers can break the magic circle, or immersion, created by the close interaction between the user and the machine. Through this break video games can make meaning which is expressed uniquely within this medium.

For Lev Manovich, author of *The Language of New Media*, the definition of new media is simple: new media is media that has been translated for use on a computer and through this translation, it becomes mutable, flowing, electronic, and composed of disparate elements that can be retranslated into a cohesive whole. The interactivity of new media, says

Manovich, is a "tautology", because the computer is inherently interactive. Instead of an internal connection of two separate symbols, like that which happens in cinema or literature, the computer asks us to physicalise this connective process.

> "Now interactive computer media asks us instead to click on an image in order to go to another image. Before we would read a sentence of a story or a line of a poem and think of other lines, images, memories. Now interactive computer media asks us to click on a highlighted sentence to go to another sentence". (Manovich, 2002, 59)

This process inherently programs the user of new media to follow the pre-connected paths of the designer of the new media. The paths of connection in new media are limited, as limited as the possible views presented by the filmmaker in cinema, but the user of new media is set apart from the audience member of cinema by his physical agency. The simple act of "clicking" is the defining element of new media.

Video games are a form of new media, and in some ways they provide the purest form of the elements of new media that I wish to address. As Alexander Galloway writes in *Gaming: Essays on Algorithmic Culture*, "With video games, the work itself is material action. One *plays* a game". (Galloway, 2006, 2) Without physical action on the part of the user, games do not exist. The user's interaction with a game is critical in its conception of form. While the viewer in the auditorium has the agency to direct his or her gaze however he or she wishes, even allowing the spectator to get up and exit the theater, the film continues unabated. In a game and in new media in general, the narrative forms wait for the interaction of the user before proceeding with a continued narrative. Even though the action in the game is scripted and the gaze of the user is as controlled as so in theater, there is a literal tactility that is absent from cinema. Cinema gives way to an almost pure scopophilic and narcissistic enjoyment in an unfolding story. (Mulvey, 1989, 18) New media has a different enjoyment, that of tactile engagement and the enforcement of agency in a digital world.

This is perhaps akin to what Anna Everett, author of *Digitextuality and Click Theory,* calls "click fetish".

> "I propose fetishising of the word click, and its attendant iconography...operate through new media's lure of a sensory plentitude presumably available simply, instantaneously, and pleasurably with any one of several clicking apparatuses". (Everett, 2003, 14)

This tactile and simple assertion of agency in a digital world is a strong source of pleasure for the user, in addition to the scopophillic and narcissistic elements seen in cinema and games. This pleasure and assertion of agency *within* a digital world is what separates the new medial click from the click of a television remote control. While television has some similarities with new media, for there is a tactile control of the media in television as well, the tactile nature of the remote control doesn't provide an image to image or sentence to sentence connective process.

In literature, there is this tactile and meaningful connection with the work. After all, the story cannot continue until an active participation with the reader is attained. Even tactily, there is an agency of the reader: turning pages and feeling the paper and cover in the hands. For the story to continue, the reader must turn the page and must connect the words and symbols on the page to each other and to past experience. The reader enters into the world, written by the author and existent entirely for the reader. However, in games and perhaps new media in general, this connection is not the same as immersion. As Jon Dovey and Helen W. Kennedy explain in *Game Cultures: Computer Games as New Media:*

> "…the immersion of a computer game player is less the submersion in virtual reality as the quality of intense concentration produced by having to attend to the combination of activities described … mastering control systems, figuring out the gameplay, puzzle solving, enemy slaying, and strategic planning". (Dovey and Kennedy, 2006, 8)

In games the immersion, is not complete, but is a complex connection between the user, a person engaged with a machine, and the machine, what Galloway calls "[T]he electronic computational device" (Galloway, 2006, 2) and refers to any device upon which a game is being played.

Katie Salen and Eric Zimmerman, the authors of *Rules of Play: Game Design Fundamentals*, describe the connection created by the interaction between user and machine as the "magic circle". The player of a game accepts certain rules and tropes of the game and challenges presented by the game designer. "The fact that the magic circle is just that – a circle – is an important feature of this concept. As a closed circle, the space it circumscribes is enclosed and separate from the real world" (Salen and Zimmerman, 2004, 95). This circle acts like immersion, but where the participant of old media is caught up in story and plot, the participant of the game is subject to the rules for interaction between the user and the machine. This circle is not as cordoned off as Salen and Zimmerman present it. T. L. Taylor, in *Play Between Worlds*, points out that this circle is not closed and the influences of the real world play a part within the game world, especially within online game worlds: "We find people negotiating levels of self –disclosure and performance, multiple forms of embodiment, the integration of dual (or multiple) communities, webs of technologies, and the importing of meaningful offline issues and values into online spaces". Where the magic circle differs in regards to immersion is that the magic circle is defined by a series of rules for interaction, and by using these rules, the user can interact with the machine. While there are definitely immersive elements in the magic circle, you can certainly be swept away by a game, the magic circle is distinguished by the notion of user-machine interaction or gameplay.

Gameplay is the social interaction that exists between the user and the machine. At its most basic level it is the simple click of the mouse connecting the pre-linked images and words together. At its most complex it can be several users communicating through a machine within a persistent virtual world, like any MMORPG, or Massive Multiplayer Online Role Playing Game. It is upon this interaction, within and without the magic circle, and not placed *solely* upon its old medial elements, that critique and theory of new media could be based. Dovey and Kennedy give their definition of Gameplay: "The "text", if we are to use that term at all, becomes the complex interaction between player and game – or what is described as *gameplay*" (Dovey and Kennedy, 2006, 6) However within game design there seems to be general misunderstanding of what games are, and more importantly, what games could be. It is these fundamental and flexible differences of gameplay that allow for the exploration of a new kind of audience interaction. Not only must those who critique games be aware of this fundamental nature of games, but game designers should be aware of it too. In incorporating the ways that people interact with the machine with the design of the game a new engagement with an audience can spring forth. If, as T.L. Taylor specifies in *Play Between Worlds,* "…players *already are* core actors in the maintenance and life of the game" (Taylor, 2006, 159) then it is upon this action that more theory and design could be based; where the spectator is not confined to merely a visually and mentally active role, but a physically active one as well.

Could this physical activity be the source of theoretical engagement with a peace of art? I find parallels between the theater of the 1940s as presented by Bertolt Brecht and the ways that video games are viewed as pure entertainment today. Brecht in *A Short Organum for the Theater* describes the state of the audience in 1947:

> "Seeing and hearing are activities, and can be pleasant ones, but these people seem relieved of activity and like men whom something is being done. This detached state, where they seem to be given over to vague but profound sensations, grows deeper the better the work of the actors, and so we, as we do not approve of this situation, should like them to be as bad as possible" (Brecht, 1947, 187)

What Brecht describes here is a complete immersion in the plot and narrative being displayed on stage, but instead of an objective engagement with the story, there is a mindless, passive engagement with the actors on stage. To remedy this Brecht calls for a theater that "not only releases the feelings and impulses possible within the particular historical field of human relations in which the action takes place, but employs and encourages those thoughts and feelings which help transform the field itself" (Brecht, 1947, 190). In order to accomplish his goal he calls upon several techniques to relate what is happening on stage to the audience. The foremost of which is the alienation effect, or A-effect.

The Brechtian A-effect tries to separate the audience from the familiar tropes of the theater and break the immersion of the audience just enough to make them realize their relation to the people on stage and make objective insights as to the purpose of the piece. This is done by having the actor be aware of his position in relation to the audience and, instead of becoming the object of spectation fully, guides the audience to meaning. (Brecht, 1947, 193) For example, if an actor is playing King Lear, he does not fully become the character because the audience would become lost in the story, instead the actor shows the audience the tribulations of Lear so that the audience understands that these tribulations are not unique to Lear and can be felt by anyone. This forces the audience to consider the deeper meanings of the play. (Brecht, 1947, 193-194)

Much like the observations Brecht made so too can the designer conscious of this interaction between the user and the machine, make strides to break the insipid world created by the separation between the real world and virtual one created by the magic circle. Like the theater in 1947, the mindset of a game player is one of entertainment, not art, and, like the audience member, the player lets the visual medium of the game simply entertain without allowing the meanings that can be present in the game relate back to the life of the player. So, perhaps the A-effect could be used in game design to break the magic circle of the game world.

In gameplay, however, this goal is more difficult to accomplish, for the relation to reality is more difficult to establish in a medium marked by its desire to separate the real from the virtual. If the user is using the game world simply for her or his own pleasure, as Dovey and Kennedy suggest, then the placement of the A-effect must be used to alienate the user from the game controls and rules. The alienation that occurs must disrupt, not the visual spectation, as what would happen in theater or cinema, but the gameplay. This is not to say that visual alienation cannot occur in games and have effect, but without a tactile disruption the alienation does not rest upon the fundamental characteristic of new media. The art of game design should not only rest upon the beauty of the game's cut scenes where the game relies on an old medial pleasure to reward the player, but upon the way the gameplay causes a distinct realization within the user, exposing the experience of the game and breaking the magic circle. There are some games out there which have come close to this ideal and I will address some of them to hope to clarify what it is I am looking for in game design.

Electroplankton (Indies Zero, 2006) is a game released for the Nintendo DS mobile gaming platform by the interactive media artist Toshio Iwai. The game consists of several games/levels/modes wherein you "control" small electric animals with the DS systems stylus and touch screen. These electric plankton move in correspondence with the touch of the user producing lights and sound. Partially controlled by the user and partially controlled by the device the user and machine enter a kind of dance, where each user action informs a computer action and the result is a ballet of lights, movement, and sound. Unlike other games the goal of this game is creation of a unique, but controlled, musical piece. The user and the machine act like partners in order to create a shared work of art, but this act of creation is not limited to the screen or in flashing colors and lights. The creation of the game is also in the invoking of movement within the user. Although the movement of the body required in for the game is localized in the hand, the movement can spread, driven by the sounds being generated by the game and by the fact that the device itself is small and hand held. The physical interaction with the game spreads through the stylus into the software where the digital creatures mimic the actions of the user. If desired, the game system could be physically set down, listened to, or changed by the user. The user and the game become embodied wholly in/of themselves and so the movement of the hand and the clicking of the stylus on the screen expose a direct interaction between the user and the machine as distinct entities.

Here a new kind a physical interaction is expressed, similar, yet distinct from the physicality of theater or literature. Not only is there a narrative play taking place, but a striving toward an end goal of creation: "Instead of a consumer, reader, or receiver, a *gamer* is more of a composer than anything else". (Dreunen, 2008, 9) This composition can exist in many forms, both vocally as seen in *Electroplankton* and textually as seen in many open world games, user-creation oriented games, and even strict narrative oriented titles.

> "An important reality of digitextuality is that the apparatuses of click – the primal interfaces granting access to cyberspace, computer-enhanced television, pocket computers, wireless and handheld devices – *always return us to the body activating and making sense of the interface*". (Everett, 2003, 25)

Electroplankton seeks to make us aware of this embodiment where the body of the user and the digital body of the on screen creature are relative to the action taking place. This causes a break in the simple pleasure of clicking and makes us aware of the machine, ourselves, and relation between them. I applaud *Electroplankton's* ability to create this break subtly, but there seems to be a lack here, for while we are made aware of ourselves in relation to the device, little is learned from it, and it is simple to slip back into the simple pleasure of playing with the device.

This is the dangerous road that the gimmick occupies. The Nintendo Wii, released 2006, is an innovative game console allowing player hand movements to interact with the characters on screen. It did well selling over 44 million copies worldwide. Its unique controls allow for a user to actually perform some of the hand gestures and movements associated with the actions taking place in the digital world. This can cause the same split that was caused in *Electroplankton*, allowing the user to become aware of the actions that he or she is performing. However with games such as Wii Fit (Nintendo EAD, 2008) where the user of the game exercises to the digital game world bodies on screen, and Wii Yoga (Tivola, 2009) where the user performs yoga to the instruction of an on screen instructor the Wiimote, or motion sensitive controller, is used to monitor the user not to engage with them. With these games and games like them the rules were not created by a designer hoping to explore intention, or through movement create and explore, the movement here has purpose, to exercise, and as such may not fit the definition of "game". There is no magic circle to break here; the actions of the user would be the same if they were working with an instructor or to a video. We can learn things from these games, but they are skills, not self-exploration.

Even without innovative controls or an emphasis on creation there is another way for games to break the magic circle: it can happen in the marriage of game controls and narrative. In *Call of Duty 4* (Infinity Ward, 2007) a well-received First Person Shooter (FPS), the standard uses of the genre are in effect. The user interacts with his environment as if he or she were actually in that situation, the user's actions mitigated to the machine through the use of the controller. Sympathy, or lack thereof, is built for the characters through previous interaction with the environment within the game. While the story primarily serves as a vessel to link action sequences together, the story at one particular point suddenly invokes itself and forces the user to step back and consider his actions within the game. The user plays as an American soldier, in a Middle Eastern country, who is suddenly caught in a nuclear explosion. Rather than showing the user what happens to the on-screen avatar with a cut scene the game forces the user to control Sergeant Paul Jackson as he crawls through a blast torn city as he slowly bleeds out. In an almost cruel way, the user suddenly becomes aware of moral implications of the actions that he has been taking in the game as well as the comment on warfare in general. By making the user play the last moment of a dying man we are made to experience the loss, rather than distance ourselves from it. The interactive tools with which the user is engaging with the environment are removed and it is in this loss that the realization of the meaning behind the story is allowed to connect with the player. By limiting, not removing, the apparatus through which the user interacts with the game, the user breaks from the game and feels an approximation of the gravity that a nuclear blast in a populated area causes.

This exploration of Brechtian alienation in games I believe can lead to a discussion of games as a form of art, unique in its structure and purpose, but there is a questioning of whether or not gaming culture would want this shift to occur. There is a prevailing viewpoint that games are produced commercially and for pure entertainment value. As Scott Rettburg insists in *Corporate Ideology in World of Warcraft*, "Video games are primarily entertainment products, not forms of art. Each type of video game and computer game is developed with an idea in mind of how to most effectively extract money from its players and provide a reliable income stream for its producers" (Rettburg, 2008, 20). Rettburg goes on to say that even in video game roots, when arcade games were designed to get as many coins from as many players as possible, and this trend has not changed, as World of Warcraft is designed to have players spend as much time as possible exploring online digital worlds, living a capitalist fantasy, and thus extracting as much money as possible from monthly subscribers. (Rettburg, 2008, 20-21) It is probably this trend of strong economic purpose that makes Roger Ebert feel that games cannot be considered high Art, the remark that sparked so much controversy in the gamer community. (Ebert, 2007)

While the common desire of game companies is to make a purchasable commodity this does not limit the possibility of art. Art is constructed by a mode of viewing based upon social construction created by the very commoditization that condemns the game community. John Berger points out that art is a form of looking, and by framing an object we create Art. According to Berger, the vocabulary formed around oil paintings between 1500 and 1900 informs many of our cultural assumptions about how we discuss art and about what art can be about. Many of these paintings, however, were created specifically as commodities: "Before they were anything else, they are themselves objects which can be bought and owned". (Berger, 1977, 85) Paintings in this time period were bought from artists specifically as a way of showing class and wealth; they were not only seen as art but as symbols of class. Berger points out that as time passed art was no longer a commodity of class, and so art became Art: "In the end, the art of the past is being mystified because a privileged minority is striving to invent a history which can retrospectively justify the role of the ruling classes, and such a justification can no longer make sense in modern terms. And so, inevitably, it mystifies". (Berger, 1977, 85) The rules that were set in place in oil painting specifically to display the wealth of the painting's owner, now serves to elevate the artwork to a mystical place of honor. If these commoditized objects are seen as Art then the commoditized spectacle of the game can be seen as Art also. However there needs to be a desire within the gaming community to want to see games as art and there should be some intention on the part of the designer to address the user of the game and not just his wallet.

I believe that there is a movement within the gaming community toward these ideals. Recently, perhaps due to the ease of downloading games through the internet, an "indie" game community has sprung up which, in part, is discussing the possibilities of games. Indie game developers are generally single or small groups of independent game designers who generally pull together for a single project. Recently the Indie developer Tale of Tales released a title called *The Path* which specifically addresses the concept of rules within game worlds. In the game you play as a version of red riding hood who is given the specific instructions to follow the path to grandma's house, and above all to not stray from the path. If the player follows the instructions and stays on the path, Red makes it to grandma's house and the game ends. The narrative created is simple and uninteresting, nothing is learned or felt by the player and the game itself tells you that you have lost. However if the player leaves the path, what ensues is a dark exploration into the brutal stories of these characters, each who suffers at the hands of a particular "wolf" and then ends with a nightmare sequence at grandma's house. Then the game ends, you win, and one of the "Reds", a character with which you can play through the game, vanishes. Here gameplay serves as a structural exploration of a game's rules. The rules in *The Path* serve to keep your character safe and alive, but ultimately lead to defeat, but in "disobeying" the rules given to the character, you are given "victory," but loose agency in the game world when you lose the character. What results is a tension between what you are expected to do, what you want to do, and what you are told to do. Much like the character Red from the Grimm fairy tale, we are drawn from the path in order to discover the pleasure of the game, but then our on screen persona are punished for giving in to this desire. The viewer becomes alienated from the game by this indecision and is forced to conceptualize his or her place within the rules and how our actions determine the course of our lives. Rules vs. consequences; Pleasure vs. punishment.

Whether or not the gaming community would like to see their favorite past time become a form of art, does not prevent the ever changing way in which media interacts with us. As new media continues to grow as a medium our interaction with it becomes ingrained: "It seems that even consumer mastery of digital media's requisite multitasking behaviors and composite text challenges accepted theories of cognition and spectatorship" (Everett, 2003, 8). As users become more adept at translating and adjusting the inherent text in New Media, the user adapts to the medium and learns to better speak and act with the machine. Everett calls this *fundamental hyperattentiveness,* and it implies a new understanding of how media is to be looked at and interacted with on a textual level. Manovich noticed this trend as well stating that "Interactive media ask us to identify with someone else's mental structure. If the cinema viewer, male and female, lusted after and tried to emulate the body of the movie star, the computer user is asked to follow the mental trajectory of the new media designer". (Manovich, 2002, 59) As people interact with new media they grow accustomed to how new media works, feels, and acts. As a result the medium starts to feel less like an alien manner of comprehension but an accepted norm. The desire to express oneself within this new way of forming meaning will prove to be unavoidable. The technologies that these forms of communication exist upon are not going away and the way that we interact with them is unique from other forms of media. The study of how we make meaning within this form is fundamental in our understanding of how we interact with technology, through technology, and with each other.

Acknowledgements

I wish to thank Chris McGahan, Dominica Brennacer, Mihoby Rabehrison, Bo Young Kim, Rayya El Zein, Kira Alker, Becca Waldo, and Kristin Wyatt Juhrs for their help in editing and critiquing this document.

References

Aarseth, Espen "Computer Game Studies, Year One". *Game Studies: The International Journal of Computer Game Research.* Volume 1, issue 1 (July, 2001) http://www.gamestudies.org/0101/editorial.html2001.

Brecht, Bertolt, "A Short Organum for the Theater" in *Brecht on Theater: The Development of an Esthetic,* edited and translated by John Willet, 91-99 New York: Hill and Wang, 1986.

Berger, John. *Ways of Seeing.* New York: British Broadcasting Corporation and Penguin Books, 1977.

Dovey, Jon and Helen W. Kennedy. *Game Cultures: Computer Games as New Media.* New York: Open University Press, 2006.

Dreunen, Joost van. "The Aesthetic Vocabulary of Video Games," *Computer Games as a Sociocultural Phenomenon: Games Without Frontiers War Without Tears* (2008): 3-11.

Ebert, Roger. "Games vs. Art: Ebert vs. Barker." *RogerEbert.com.* (July 21, 2007). http://rogerebert.suntimes.com/apps/pbcs.dll/article?AID=/20070721/COMMENTARY/70721001

Everett, Anna. "Digitextuality and Click Theory," *New Media: Theories and Practices* (2003): 3-28.

Galloway, Alexander R. *Gaming: Essays on Algorythmic Culture*. Minneapolis: University of Minnesota Press, 2006.

Indies Zero. (2006). *Electroplankton.* [Nintendo DS], Japan: Nintendo

Infinity Ward. (2007). *Call of Duty 4: Modern Warfare.* [Playstation 3], USA: Activision.

Kojima Productions. (2008). *Metal Gear Solid 4: Guns of the Patriots.* [Playstation 3], Japan: Konami.

Manovich, Lev. *The Language of New Media.* Cambridge: MIT Press, 2002.

Mulvey, Laura. *Visual and Other Pleasures.* Indianapolis, IN: Indiana University Press, 1989.

Rettburg, Scott. "Corporate Ideology in World of Warcraft," *Digital Culture, Play, and Identity: a World of Warcraft Reader* (2008): 20-21.

Salen, Katie, and Eric Zimmerman. *Rules of Play: Game Design Fundamentals*. Cambridge: MIT Press, 2004.

Taylor, T.L. *Play Between Worlds: Exploring Online Game Culture.* Cambridge: MIT press, 2006.

Valve Corporation. (2004). *Half-Life* 2. [PC], USA: Sierra Entertainment.

CONTRIBUTORS

Isabelle Choinière

In 2005, Isabelle Choinière began a doctorate at the Centre for Advanced Inquiry in the Interactive Arts (CAiiA) affiliated with Plymouth University in England, under the supervision of Roy Ascott, founder and director of the Planetary Collegium. Founder and director of *Corps Indice* in Montreal, Canada, a company working with the relationship between dance and technology, Isabelle Choinière's research looks into the ways in which the infiltration of technological thought in actual dance/performance may find applications in the development of new choreographic models. Since 1995, she has regularly presented her creations and lectures in international festivals (France, Germany, Denmark, the Canary Islands, Spain, Brazil, Mexico, Chili, Argentina, Canada). Her works are studied by numerous research groups and universities throughout the world; her latest articles have been published by the University of Applied Arts Vienna (Austria) and will be published in 2010 in the book *POINT OF BEING*, under the direction of Derrick de Kerckhove.
URL: www.isabellechoiniere.com

Kazuhiro Jo

Kazuhiro Jo is an artist and researcher in the fields of sound art and interactive media educated at Kyushu Institute of Design and the University of Tokyo. He has exhibited and performed internationally at DEAF'04 (Dutch Electronic Art Festival), NTT InterComunicationCenter, Yokohama International Triennale 2005, ISEA (International Syposium of Electronic Arts) 2006. His work is interdisciplinary, crossing boundaries of interaction design, sound art, and the DIY (Do It Yourself) ethic. He is a practitioner, writer, and organizer. His artistic work includes participatory sound performances, sensor based musical instruments, and image-sound processing software platforms. He is a researcher on the EPSRC funded Social Inclusion through the Digital Economy (SIDE) project at Newcastle University, specialised in deploying mobile interactive music technologies with regional youth groups.

Stephan Ferdinand Jürgens
INET-MD – Centro de Estudos de Música e Dança / Centre for Music and Dance Studies.

Stephan Ferdinand Jürgens holds a Master's in Contemporary Performing Arts and is currently concluding his PhD on Contemporary Choreography and New Media Technologies. His research interests concentrate on designing creative strategies for live performance involving interactive systems. He has been teaching movement research, interdisciplinary choreography and interactive system design in many different learning environments and institutions for many different people ranging from interested beginners to professional performers and MA students.

He collaborated on several international research projects, such as Eurodans.net and TeDance, and was co-ordinator of the Get-Real-Project, all of which investigated the use recent technology in Contemporary Dance and Live Performance. As a choreographer he has presented several works supported by the Portuguese Ministry of Culture. He is an author of several papers in international and national publications.

Michael Takeo Magruder
Michael Takeo Magruder is an artist and researcher in King's Visualisation Lab, based in the Centre for Computing in the Humanities, King's College London. His work has been showcased in over 200 exhibitions and 30 countries, and uses emerging technologies, including high-performance computing, mobile devices and virtual environments to explore the networked, digital world.

Dr Frank Millward
Dr Frank Millward is a multimedia artist, composer / performer.
His creative work and research explores cross-disciplinary relationships between technology, science and art where focus is given to the ways in which sound and moving image are shaping new interactive communicative forms in live and virtual environs. He lectures and presents workshops in audio art, sound design and the moving image, interdisciplinary project management, music and multimedia composition at the School of Fine Art, Faculty of Art, Design & Architecture, Kingston University, London.
URLs: www.frankmillward.com and www.thevisualvoice.co.uk

Carla Montez Fernandes

Carla Montez Fernandes graduated in Modern Languages and Literatures (English/German studies) and holds a Master's and PhD in Linguistics. She is a Professor at *IPLeiria* and currently Senior Researcher at *CLUNL - Universidade Nova de Lisboa*. She coordinates the recently state-funded **TKB** project (a Transmedia Knowledge- Base for contemporary dance) with international partners such as the University of Amsterdam and Ohio State University.

At present her research focus is in the intersection of Cognitive Linguistics and the Performative Arts, particularly concerning the creation of multimodal digital archives. She works as scientific consultant for several contemporary dance companies and is research partner of the Amsterdam-based international project "*Inside Movement Knowledge*", on invitation by Scott DeLahunta and Bertha Bermudez, at the crossing of arts, science and practice since September 2008.

Co-author of *Oxford/Verbo English-Portuguese Dictionary* (1997); author of chapters in books and several papers in international and national publications.

Lisa Newman

Lisa Newman is an intermedia performance artist and co-director/ founder of 2 Gyrlz Performative Arts. She received a BS in Fine Art from the University of Oregon in 1996, and an MA in Performance and Cultural Location in Contemporary Europe from Dartington College of Art in Devon, UK in 2007. Newman will be beginning a PhD in Performance Studies at the University of Manchester in September of 2009.
URL: www.2gyrlz.org

Rachel O'Dwyer

Rachel O'Dwyer holds an undergraduate degree in Fine Art, and recently graduated with an M.Phil in Music and Media Technologies from Trinity College Dublin (TCD). She is currently undertaking a PHD in the Engineering Department of TCD on mobile media and urban planning and is funded by the Irish Research Council for Science, Engineering and Technology. She is an associate researcher with the Graduate School of Creative Arts and Media in Dublin (GradCam).

Alain B. Renaud

After several years working as a sound engineer, composer and music industry consultant, Alain Renaud completed his PhD at the Sonic Arts

Research Centre (SARC), Queen's University Belfast in 2009. Alain was appointed lecturer at Bournemouth University in November 2008.

His research focuses on the development of networked music performance systems with an emphasis on the creation of strategies to interact over a network musically and the notion of shared networked acoustic spaces. He performs regularly over the network with the NetVs.Net collective (www.netvsnet.com) and has performed and presented his research in various places, such as the Banff Centre for the Art, The Center for Computer Research in Music and Acoustics (CCRMA) at Stanford University, where he was a visiting scholar in 2007 and various conferences, including New Interfaces for Musical Expression (NIME), the International Computer Music Conference (ICMC) and the Audio Engineering Society (AES). He is also involved as an advisor in the EU network performance project, CoMeDia (www.comedia.eu.org).

He is to co-direct the Sounding Out International conference at Bournemouth University in 2010. In his spare time, he has been producing music for the Montreux Jazz Festival (www.montreuxjazz.com) since 1997.

URL: www.alainrenaud.net

Franziska Schroeder

Franziska Schroeder is a saxophonist and theorist. From 2007 - 2009 she was an AHRC, UK Research Fellow in the Creative and Performing Arts. Franziska is now a Lecturer/RCUK Fellow at the Sonic Arts Research Centre, Queen's University Belfast.

URL: www.sarc.qub.ac.uk/~fschroeder

Blog: http://lautnet.blogspot.com

Atau Tanaka

Atau Tanaka holds the Chair of Digital Media at Newcastle University. He holds degrees from Harvard University, and Stanford University's CCRMA. He has worked at IRCAM in Paris, and as Artistic Ambassador for Apple France. In 2001 he was the first artist to become researcher at Sony Computer Science Laboratory Paris. Atau's work bridges the fields of interactive media and computer music. He holds a patent on musical control interfaces using physiological biosignals. He seeks to harness collective musical creativity in mobile environments, seeking out the continued place of the artist in democratized digital forms. His work has received awards from Ars Electronica, Fondation Langlois, and the Fraunhofer Institute and has been funded by Research Councils UK (AHRC, EPSRC), the French National Research Agency (ANR), and the

Japanese Ministry of Telecommunications. He has been mentor at NESTA and is currently Acting Director of Culture Lab.

Desmond Traynor

Desmond Traynor is a graduate of University College Dublin and Trinity College Dublin, and a Hennessy Short Story Award winner, whose novel *The Myth of Exile and Return* was nominated for the 2005 Hughes & Hughes/*Sunday Independent* Irish Novel of the Year Award. He teaches Contemporary Fiction and Postcolonial Theory and Literature in the School of Arts, Dublin Business School, and Creative Writing in the Irish Writers' Centre and Rathmines College of Further Education. He is working on a doctorate at the Clinton Institute for American Studies, UCD, on dissent in popular music. He gratefully acknowledges the assistance of the Dr Ciaran Barry Research Scholarship.

Simon Waters

Director of Research, Head of Electroacoustic Studios & Senior Lecturer in Music, University of East Anglia

Simon Waters is a musician whose practice has shifted from studio-based acousmatic composition (in the 1980s) to a position which reflects his sense that music is primarily concerned with human action, and only secondarily with acoustic fact. Clearly-defined compositions have increasingly been replaced by performances which bring together particular sets of strategies, technologies, performers and environments. His research investigates the relationship between music and other activities, contiguities between performing and composing/improvising, 'instrument building', and the manner in which musical thought and practice operate in highly technologised contexts. As Director of the Electroacoustic Music Studios at the University of East Anglia he curates the long-running Sonic Arts concert series and programmes guest seminars, workshops and residencies at UEA, in the UK, and abroad. He has an international reputation as an electroacoustic composer, with awards and commissions in the UK and abroad, and speaks regularly at conferences (not always on music). He has worked with many contemporary dance and physical theatre companies and visual artists including Ballet Rambert, Adventures in Motion Pictures and the Royal Opera House Garden Venture, and multimedia theatre practitioners Moving Being. His works have been widely presented and broadcast in the UK, Europe and the USA.

Contact: s.waters@uea.ac.uk

Dane White

Dane White holds a master's degree from New York University, TISCH: School of the Arts in Performance Studies and a bachelor's degree in Anthropology and Theater from Illinois Wesleyan University. He is currently working on his dissertation proposal for a degree in games studies.